Workshop on Natural Language Processing for Social Media 2013

(SocialNLP)

AA004631

Held at the 6th International Joint Conference on Natural Language Processing (IJCNLP 2013)

Nagoya, Japan
14-18 October 2013

ISBN: 978-1-62993-542-3

Printed from e-media with permission by:

Curran Associates, Inc.
57 Morehouse Lane
Red Hook, NY 12571

CURRAN ASSOCIATES INC. proceedings.com

Some format issues inherent in the e-media version may also appear in this print version.

Copyright© (2013) by the Association for Computational Linguistics
All rights reserved.

Printed by Curran Associates, Inc. (2014)

For permission requests, please contact the Association for Computational Linguistics at the address below.

Association for Computational Linguistics
209 N. Eighth Street
Stroudsburg, Pennsylvania 18360

Phone: 1-570-476-8006
Fax: 1-570-476-0860

acl@aclweb.org

Additional copies of this publication are available from:

Curran Associates, Inc.
57 Morehouse Lane
Red Hook, NY 12571 USA
Phone: 845-758-0400
Fax: 845-758-2634
Email: curran@proceedings.com
Web: www.proceedings.com

Table of Contents

Sixth International Joint Conference on
Natural Language Processing

IJCNLP2013
THE 6TH INTERNATIONAL JOINT CONFERENCE ON
NATURAL LANGUAGE PROCESSING
OCTOBER 14–18, 2013
NAGOYA CONGRESS CENTER, NAGOYA, JAPAN

Proceedings of the Workshop on Natural Language Processing for Social Media (SocialNLP)

Introduction

Welcome to the IJCNLP 2013 Workshop on Natural Language Processing for Social Media (SocialNLP). SocialNLP is a new inter-disciplinary area of natural language processing (NLP) and social computing. We consider three plausible directions of SocialNLP: (1) addressing issues in social computing using NLP techniques; (2) solving NLP problems using information from social networks or social media; and (3) handling new problems related to both social computing and natural language processing.

Through this workshop, we anticipate to provide a platform for research outcome presentation and head-to-head discussion in the area of SocialNLP, with the hope to combine the insight and experience of prominent researchers from both NLP and social computing domains to contribute to the area of SocialNLP jointly. Also, we have come to an agreement with International Journal of Computational Linguistics and Chinese Language Processing (IJCLCLP) to select some high quality papers from SocialNLP to publish in this journal.

The submissions to this year workshop were again of high quality and we had a competitive selection process. We received 19 submissions, and due to a rigorous review process, we only accept 6 of them. Thus the acceptance rate is 31%. The accepted papers cover a broad range of SocialNLP-related topics, such as audience prediction, sentiment analysis, metaphor detection, opinion mining, and trust evaluation. We have totally 20 reviewers. We appreciate our PC members for the timely reviews and constructive comments.

We are delighted to have Prof. Yohei Seki, from University of Tsukuba, as our keynote speaker.

We especially thanks the Workshop Committee Chairs Prof. Naoaki Okazaki and Dr. Scott Wen-tau Yih.

We hope you enjoy the workshop!

The workshop organizers
Shou-de Lin, Lun-Wei Ku, and Tsung-Ting Kuo
October 14, 2013
Nagoya, Japan

Organizers:

Shou-de Lin, National Taiwan University
Lun-Wei Ku, Academia Sinica
Tsung-Ting Kuo, National Taiwan University

Program Committee:

Chia-Hui Chang, National Central University
Berlin Chen, National Taiwan Normal University
Min-Yuh Day, Tamkang University
Jennifer Foster, Dublin City University
Wen-Lian Hsu, Academia Sinica
June-Jei Kuo, National Chung Hsing University
Chuan-Jie Lin, National Taiwan Ocean University
Yohei Seki, University of Tsukuba
Ker-Yi Su, Behavior Design Corp
Ming-Feng Tsai, National ChengChi University
Hsin-Min Wang, Academia Sinica
Jenq-Haur Wang, National Taipei University of Technology
Shih-Hung Wu, Chaoyang University of Technology
Yungfang Wu, Peking University
Ruifeng Xu, Harbin Institute of Technology Shenzhen Graduate School
Yi-Hsuan Yang, Academia Sinica
Kevin Zhang, Beijing Institute of Technology

Conference Program

Monday October 14, 2013 13:30 - 16:40 R221

(13:30) Opening

(13:35) Keynote Speech: Facilitating Social Communication Using Collaborative Annotation Data, by Prof. Yohei Seki, University of Tsukuba

(14:15) Oral Presentation 1

Predicting TV Audience Rating with Social Media
Wen-Tai Hsieh, Seng-cho T. Chou, Yu-Hsuan Cheng and Chen-Ming Wu

S-Sense: A Sentiment Analysis Framework for Social Media Sensing
Choochart Haruechaiyasak, Alisa Kongthon, Pornpimon Palingoon and Kanokorn Trakultaweekoon

Social Metaphor Detection via Topical Analysis
Ting-Hao Huang

(15:15) Break

(15:35) Oral Presentation 2

The New Eye of Government: Citizen Sentiment Analysis in Social Media
Ravi Arunachalam and Sandipan Sarkar

Modeling the Helpful Opinion Mining of Online Consumer Reviews as a Classification Problem
Yi-Ching Zeng and Shih-Hung Wu

Trust Evaluation Mechanisms for Wikipedia
Imran Latif and Syed Waqar Jaffry

We wish to thank our sponsors and supporters!

Platinum Sponsors

www.anlp.jp

Silver Sponsors

www.google.com

Bronze Sponsors

www.rakuten.com

Supporters

NAGOYA CONVENTION
& VISITORS BUREAU

Nagoya Convention & Visitors Bureau

We wish to thank our organizers

Organizers

Asian Federation of Natural Language Processing (AFNLP)

Toyohashi University of Technology

Predicting TV Audience Rating with Social Media

Wen-Tai Hsieh
Institute for Information Industry
wentai@iii.org.tw

Seng-cho T. Chou
National Taiwan University
chou@im.ntu.edu.tw

Yu-Hsuan Cheng
Institute for Information Industry
joelcheng@iii.org.tw

Chen-Ming Wu
Institute for Information Industry
cmwu@iii.org.tw

Abstract

In Taiwan, there are different types of TV programs, and each program usually has its broadcast length and frequency. We accumulate the broadcasted TV programs' word-of-mouth on Facebook and apply the Back-propagation Network to predict the latest program audience rating. TV audience rating is an important indicator regarding the popularity of programs and it is also a factor to influence the revenue of broadcast stations via advertisements. Currently, the present media environments are drastically changing our media consumption patterns. We can watch TV programs on YouTube regardless location and timing. In this paper, we develop a model for predicting TV audience rating. We also present the audience rating trend analysis on demo system which is used to describe the relation between predictive audience rating and Nielsen TV rating.

1 Introduction

As social media websites develop, more and more people are sharing their thoughts on these types of websites (such as Facebook). Many enterprises noticed this trend, and started creating fan pages on Facebook to interact with the customers in order to create a simple channel for interaction to consolidate customer loyalty. Currently, many television companies have creates fan pages for shows that they are broadcasting, and use the role of editor to announce upcoming plots or actor information to interact with the viewers and get responses from them, in order to try to increase ratings; higher rates help bring in more advertising revenues for the television company.

Because these types of social media websites, such as Facebook, have already become a part of people's everyday life, this research will try to use the contents generated in the TV program fan pages by viewers and the editor (including Posts, Likes and Comments etc.) and the Artificial Neural Network to perform forecasts on program ratings. If television companies can find out ratings information in advance, they can use this as a basis to negotiate the advertising period and fees with advertisers; it can also help the television channel observe the benefits of operating program fan pages, and then decide whether to reinforce fan page management or add additional interactions with the fans and further increase ratings and profits.

This research constructed a program ratings forecast module based on Back-propagation Network. This model uses various information on fan pages of completed broadcasting programs and the actual ratings to perform the training for the Artificial Neural Network, and then uses the trained Artificial Neural network to perform a ratings forecast for upcoming programs.

2 Preliminary

2.1 Artificial Neural Network

The Artificial Neural Network uses a large number of simple artificial neurons that mimics the biological neural network's processing, transmitted and learning process and abilities in order to implement the biological neural network's information processing system. The architecture of a common 3-layered neural network is shown in the figure below:

IJCNLP 2013 Workshop on Natural Language Processing for Social Media (SocialNLP), pages 1–5,
Nagoya, Japan, 14 October 2013.

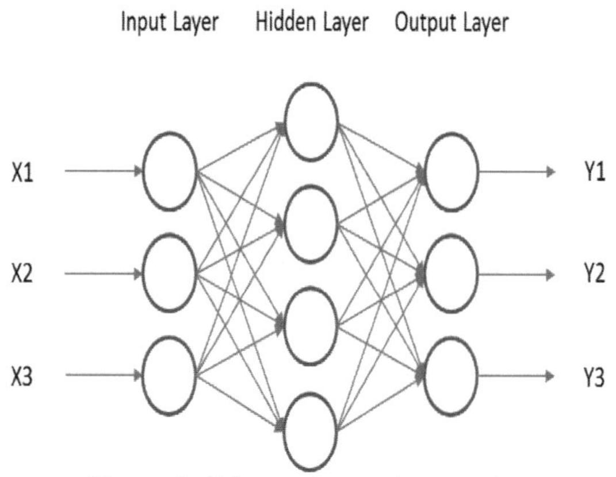

Figure 1. 3-layered neural network

The Back-propagation Network used in this research is a supervised learning network. It uses the error that each epoch generated during training, and adjusts each neuron's weight using a gradient descent to minimize training errors to adapt to the data of the training data set, and apply the unseen data to the trained network to perform a forecast. The correction method of Error is as follows:

$$w_{k+1} = w_k - \eta \sum_{t=1}^{k} \alpha^{k-t} \left(\frac{\partial \varepsilon_t}{\partial w_t} \right) \quad (1)$$

In which ε is the sum of the accumulated errors of each epoch, η is the learning rate, and in order to make the update of w more gentle and avoid oscillation, that is why α (momentum) is quoted to accelerate convergence.

Currently, many researchers has used the back-propagation method to train their network to perform forecasts; Ismail and Jamaluddin uses BPN to perform forecast to the electricity load demand, and the result showed that when Sigmoid is used as the activation function, the forecast data was closer to the actual data. Baboo and Shereef also used 3-layered back-propagation neural network to perform weather forecasts, and the result also showed that BPN has excellent generalization capacity.

2.2 Social Network

Although Facebook has been very popular as a web service, there has not been considerable published research on it. Huberman and others [2] studied the social interactions on Twitter to reveal that the driving process for usage is a sparse hidden network underlying the friends and followers, while most of the links represent meaningless interactions. Java et al [1] investigated community structure and isolated different types of user intentions on Twitter. Jansen and others have examined Twitter as a mechanism for word-of-mouth advertising, and considered articular brands and products while examining the structure of the postings and the change in sentiments. However the authors do not perform any analysis on the predictive aspect of Twitter.

3 Training Model

The sources of the data used in this research are the number of posts, likes, comments and shares etc. of each post in the various program fan pages, and the counts of these from the fan page administrators and fans were calculated separately. The data from a total of 4 fan pages were used (Office Girls, Love Forward, The Fierce Wife, and King Flower, in which King Flower is a program that is still currently airing); the ratings data of historic programs were provided by the television companies.

This research mainly focuses on a TV drama that airs once a week, and collects the number of discussions on the fan page every week and the corresponding ratings for the episode aired each week to use as the training and test data; the data includes 10 properties: #Page Posts, #Page posts comments, #Page posts likes, #page posts shares, #Fans posts, #Fans posts comments, #Fans posts likes, #Fans posts shares, previous episode TVR, and 1st episode TVR. In which, the number of comments is the number of unrepeated response count for each post, used to lower the effects on the forecast results caused by vast responses due to special events. In order for the data to be able to be used by the Back-propagation Network back-propagation, all the data were normalized before training and testing so that they are between 0 and 1, and then the data were inputted to perform training or testing. In order to acquire the 1st episode TVR, forecast was not performed for the ratings of the first episode.

In consideration of the duration of the plot being discussed in to fan page, this research used a sliding window to integrate the data to create sums of data accumulated within 3 weeks and 1 week to use as the input data.

D. Meyer & R. J. Hyndman's recommendation was used for the percentage value of TVR, and Arcsine transformation was performed to prevent heteroscedasticity from happening.

The architecture of the neural network is as shown in the figure below:

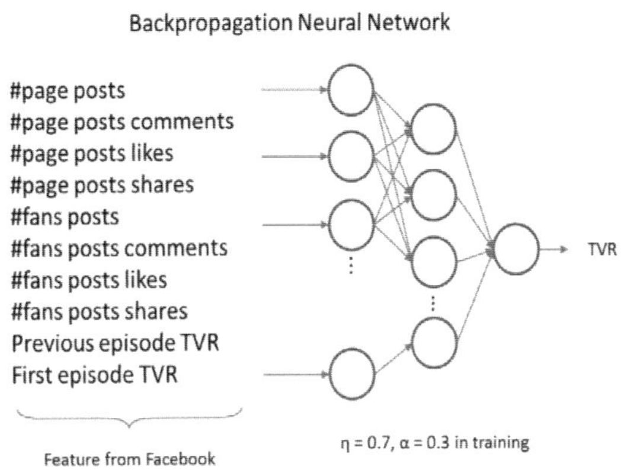

Figure 2. Training Model

4 Experiments

This research used the Cross Validation method to perform experiments. Four out of five programs were picked out every time to use as training data; 70% of the training data is used for training and 30% is used for testing. Finally, the fan page data from the last program was used to perform forecast for the ratings of every episode of the program, then use mean absolute error (MAE) and mean absolute percentage error (MAPE) to compare and evaluate the forecast model.

For learning rate (η), momentum (α) and error tolerance (τ), it was discovered after the experiment that when η=0.7,α=0.3 and τ=0.06, the forecast performance was most ideal.

The number of episodes and ratings of each program are shown in the table below:

Drama Name	*#Episode*	*Max TVR (%)*	*Min TVR (%)*
Office Girls	25	7.33	2.78
Love Forward	22	2.67	1.97
The Fierce Wife	23	9.80	0.91
King Flower	8	2.14	1.29

Table 1. Episode of each program

The forecast results of each program were measured with its Mean Absolute Error (MAE) and Mean Absolute Percentage Error (MAPE); the results are shown as in the table below (the accumulation of one week is abbreviated as C1 and the accumulation of three weeks is abbreviated as C3):

Drama Name	*MAE (C1/C3)*	*MAPE (C1/C3)*
Office Girls	0.2946 / 0.5115	5.73% / 10.47%
Love Forward	0.1775 / 0.2042	7.59% / 8.99%
The Fierce Wife	0.4090 / 0.4861	11.37% / 23.71%
King Flower	0.1969 / 0.1959	11.19% / 17.10%

Table 2. Episode of each program

MAPE(%)	*Evaluation*
MAPE ≤ 10%	High Accuracy Forecasting
10% ≤ MAPE ≤ 20%	Good Forecasting
20% ≤ MAPE ≤ 50%	Reasonable Forecasting
MAPE > 50%	Inaccurate Forecasting

Table 3. Lewis' MAPE definition

From the table above it can be seen that the performance of the value data of the accumulation of one week is better than the accumulation of three weeks; and according to Lewis' (1982) definition of the MAPE value, the performance of the value data of the accumulation of one week are all between the high accuracy forecasting and good forecasting. This shows that using the various data from fan pages to perform future ratings forecasts is feasible. The forecast table of each program is shown in the figures below:

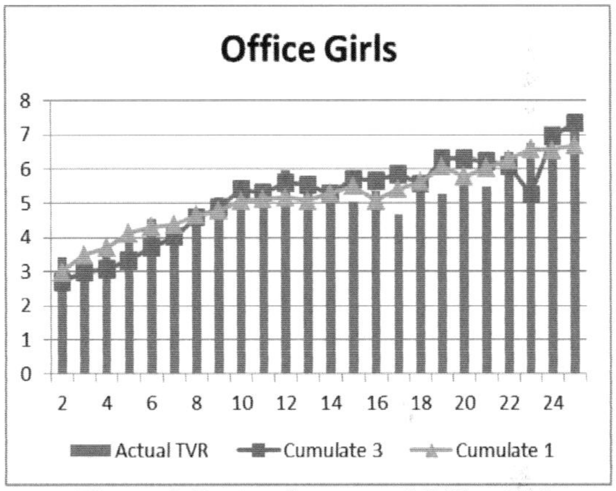

Figure 3. Rating forecast of Office Girls

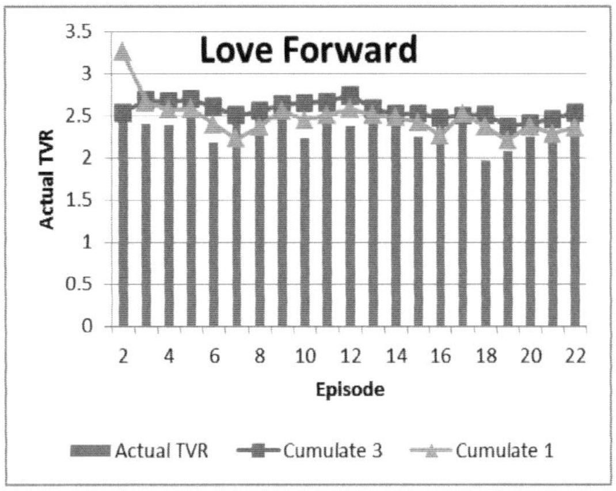

Figure 4. Rating forecast of Love Forward

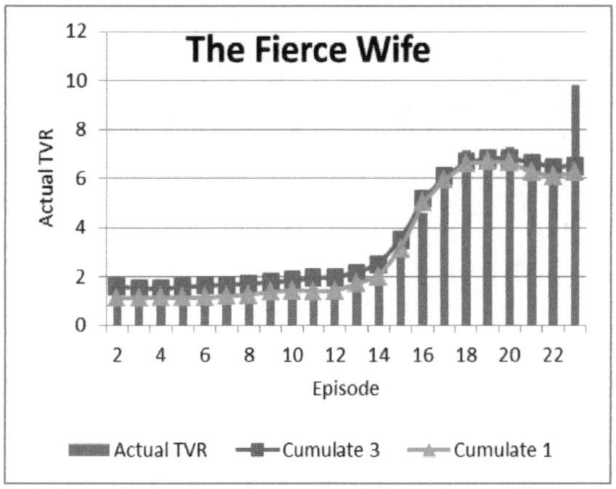

Figure 5. Rating forecast of The Fierce Wife

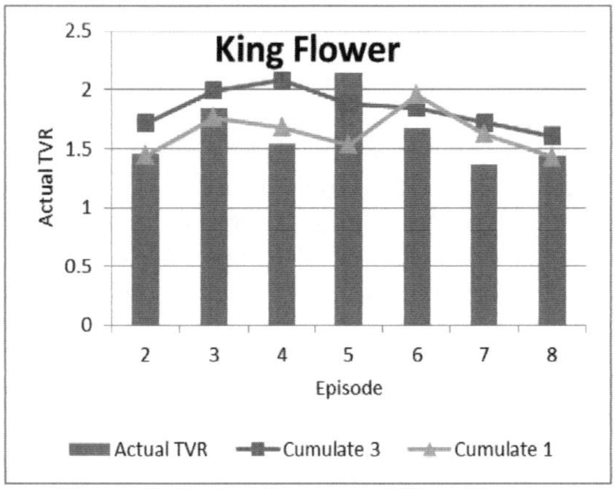

Figure 6. Rating forecast of King Flower

From the various figures above and the performance of the MAPE value, it can be seen that the results from using the Back-propagation Network back-propagation to perform forecasting matches the actual ratings in most cases, in which performance was optimal when the accumulated data of one week was used to perform the training and testing; only two sets fell between the good forecasting interval, and the rest all fell between the high accuracy forecasting interval.

5 Discussion

We also discovered some problems during the experiment process. For example, in episode 17 of Office Girls, episode 2 of Love Forward and episode 4 of King Flower, the ratings were obviously overrated; in which Office Girls and King Flower were each affected by the premiere and finale of other programs from other television companies, therefore, viewership was divided. In the future, if television companies can take the initiative to provide the current status and special events (premiere and finale) of program broadcast from other television channels, this should be able to lower this type of error. As for Love Forward, the fan page administrators posted articles such as "If you like it, then press Like/Share", resulting in the number of Likes and Shares to vastly increase and further cause the ratings to be overrated. Therefore, in the future, keyword detection for the content of these types of articles is necessary to lower the effects caused by these large amounts of Likes and Shares. In addition, the ratings of episodes 21 and 22 of Miss Rose suddenly dropped without facing premieres or finales of other programs or special events; therefore, in-depth probing for the various elements which affected their ratings is needed.

6 Conclusion

This research used the back-propagation Network and the number of posts, likes, comments and shares on the fan pages of various TV dramas to try to find their relationships to ratings. First of all, the various data information from the fan pages of 4 TV dramas were collected, and the number of repeated respondents in the same article was filtered out in order to avoid large amount of increased responses due to special events (such as quizzes or Facebook Meeting Rooms etc.) from affecting the forecast of ratings. Because the discussion of plots will not centered in one day, the sliding window method was used to generate the experiment data sets, and were divided into two data sets: the accumulation of the previous week and the accumulation of the previous three weeks. Then the data were normalized and the cross validation method was used to perform forecast module training and testing for every program. The result showed that using Facebook fan page data to perform ratings forecasts for unaired programs should be feasible.

Acknowledgments
This study is conducted under the "Social Intelligence Analysis Service Platform" project of the Institute for Information Industry which is subsidized by the Ministry of Economy Affairs of the Republic of China.

References

Akshay J., Xiaodan S., Tim F. and Belle T.. Why we twitter: understanding microblogging usage and communities. Proceedings of the 9th WebKDD and

1st SNA-KDD 2007 workshop on Web mining and social network analysis, pages 56–65, 2007

Bernardo A. Huberman, Daniel M. Romero, and Fang Wu. Social networks that matter: Twitter under the microscope. First Monday, 14(1), Jan 2009.

B. Jansen, M. Zhang, K. Sobel, and A. Chowdury. Twitter power: Tweets as electronic word of mouth. Journal of the American Society for Information Science and Technology, 2009.

Denny M. and Rob J. H.. The accuracy of television network rating forecasts: The effects of data aggregation and alternative models, Model Assisted Statistics and Applications Vol. 1, No. 3, pp.147-155, 2006.

Lewis, C. D. Industrial and Business Forecasting Method. London: Butterworth Scientific Publishers.

S. Santhosh B. and I.Kadar S.. An Efficient Weather Forecasting System using Artificial Neural Network, International Journal of Environmental Science and Development, Vol. 1, No. 4, pp. 321-326, 2010.

Zuhaimy I. and Faridatul A. J.. A Backpropagation Method for Forecasting Electricity Load Demand, Journal of Applied Sciences Vol. 8, No. 13, pp.2428-2434, 2008.

S-Sense: A Sentiment Analysis Framework for Social Media Sensing

Choochart Haruechaiyasak, Alisa Kongthon,
Pornpimon Palingoon and Kanokorn Trakultaweekoon
Speech and Audio Technology Laboratory (SPT)
National Electronics and Computer Technology Center (NECTEC)
Thailand Science Park, Klong Luang, Pathumthani 12120, Thailand
choochart.har@nectec.or.th, alisa.kon@nectec.or.th
pornpimon.pal@nectec.or.th, kanokorn.tra@nectec.or.th

Abstract

Due to the explosive growth of social media usage in Thailand, many businesses and organizations including market research agencies are seeking for tools which could perform real-time sentiment analysis on the large contents. In this paper, we propose *S-Sense*, a framework for analyzing sentiment on Thai social media. The proposed framework consists of analysis modules and language resources. Two main analysis modules, *intention* and *sentiment*, are based on classification algorithm to automatically assign appropriate intention and sentiment class labels for a given text. To train classification models, language resources, i.e., corpus and lexicon, are needed. Corpus consists of a collection of texts manually labeled with appropriate intention and sentiment classes. Lexicon consists of both general terms from dictionary and clue terms which help identifying the intention and sentiment. To evaluate performance and robustness of the analysis modules, we prepare a data set from *Twitter* posts and *Pantip* web board in mobile service domain. The experiments are set up to compare the performance between two different lexicon sets, i.e., general and clue terms. The results show that incorporating clue terms into feature vectors for constructing the classification models yield significant improvement in terms of accuracy.

1 Introduction

Due to the enormous volume, social media has become recognized as a good example of *Big Data*. One of the challenging issues in handling big data is to perform real-time analysis on the contents. Today social media has been widely accepted as an active communication channel between companies and customers. Many companies regularly use social networking websites to promote new products and services, and post announcements to the customers. On the other hand, customers often post their comments to express some sentiments towards products and services. Many customers also post questions and requests to get answers and helps from the customer services. Due to the real-time nature of the social media, monitoring customers' comments has become a critical task in customer relation management (CRM). Sentiment analysis has received much attention among market research community as an effective approach for analyzing social media contents. Some highlighted applications of sentiment analysis include brand monitoring, campaign monitoring and competitive analysis.

Thailand is among the top countries having a large population on social networking websites such as *Facebook* and *Twitter*. The recent statistics show that the number of Facebook users in Thailand has reached 17 millions as of October 29, 2012[1]. Many companies in Thailand start to see the importance of using social media analysis to gain some insight on what people think about their brands, products and services. Although many commercial software tools for social media analysis are available, they do not support Thai language. In this paper, we propose *S-Sense*, a framework for analyzing sentiment on Thai social media contents. To provide a complete solution, our proposed framework consists of many components including tagging tool, language resources, analysis and visualizing modules.

Among all of the components in S-Sense, language resources are considered very essential for providing the infrastructure to train both inten-

[1] Facebook statistics, *http://en.wikipedia.org/wiki/Facebook_statistics*

IJCNLP 2013 Workshop on Natural Language Processing for Social Media (SocialNLP), pages 6–13,
Nagoya, Japan, 14 October 2013.

tion and sentiment analysis models. In our proposed framework, language resources consist of two components, corpus and lexicon. Corpus consists of a collection of texts manually labeled with appropriate intention and sentiment classes. Lexicon consists of two types of terms, general and clue. The general lexicon includes terms found in *LEXiTRON*[2], which is a well-known Thai-English electronic dictionary. In S-Sense, the general lexicon is modified by including new terms such as slangs, chat language, transliterated words, found in Thai Twitter corpus. The second lexicon consists of clue terms which help identifying the intention and sentiment. Example of clue terms for sentiment analysis are polar terms (such as "stylish", "beautiful" and "expensive"), which contain either positive or negative sentiment.

For the analysis modules, we apply classification algorithm to automatically assign appropriate intention and sentiment class labels for a given text. The performance of classification models generally depends on the choice of classification algorithms including parameter settings, the size of training corpus and the design of term feature sets. The current version of S-Sense applies the multinomial Naive Bayes algorithm. The reason we used Naive Bayes is its requirement of a small amount of training data to estimate the parameters for learning the models. Also Naive Bayes is a descriptive and probabilistic machine learning, therefore, the results could be easily analyzed and explained. The classification results are returned with a probability value which could be interpreted as the confidence level. In addition to the proposed framework, another contribution of this paper is the comparative study of using different lexicon sets for training the analysis models. We compare the performance of intention and sentiment analysis models by using two different sets of lexicons, general and clue terms. The evaluation corpus consist of *Twitter* posts and *Pantip* web board topics in mobile service domain. The experimental results will be presented along with the discussion on the error analysis.

The remainder of this paper is organized as follows. In next section, we review some related works on sentiment analysis and many different approaches for constructing language resources for sentiment analysis. In Section 3, we present the proposed S-Sense framework for Thai intention and sentiment analysis. Details on each components are given with illustration. In Section 4, we evaluate the framework by using a data set collected from Twitter and Pantip Thai web board. Examples of difficult cases are discussed along with some possible solutions. Section 5 concludes the paper with the future work.

[2]LEXiTRON, *http://lexitron.nectec.or.th*

2 Related work

Due to its potential and useful applications, opinion mining and sentiment analysis has gained a lot of interest in text mining and NLP communities (Ding et al., 2008; Jin et al., 2009; Tsytsarau and Palpanas., 2012). Much work in this area focused on evaluating reviews as being positive or negative either at the document level (Pang et al., 2002; Beineke et al., 2004) or sentence level (Kim and Hovy, 2004; Wilson et al., 2009). For instance, given some reviews of a product, the system classifies them into positive or negative reviews. No specific details or features are identified about what customers like or dislike. To obtain such details, a *feature-based* opinion mining approach has been proposed (Hu and Liu, 2004).

The problem of developing subjectivity lexicons for training and testing sentiment classifiers has recently attracted some attention. Although most of the reference corpora has been focused on English language, work on other languages is growing as well. Ku and Chen (2007) proposed the bag-of-characters approach to determine sentiment words in Chinese. This approach calculates the observation probabilities of characters from a set of seed sentiment words first, then dynamically expands the set and adjusts their probabilities. Later in 2009, Ku et al. (2009), extended their bag-of-characters approach by including morphological structures and syntactic structures between sentence segment. Their experiments showed better performance of word polarity detection and opinion sentence extraction. Haruechaiyasak et al. (2010), proposed a framework for constructing Thai language resource for feature-based opinion mining. The proposed approach for extracting features and polar words is based on syntactic pattern analysis.

Our main contribution in this paper is the proposed framework for analyzing intention, sentiment, and language usage from social media texts. We initially performed some evaluation on Thai texts to show the effectiveness of the proposed components and modules. The proposed framework can be easily extended to support other languages, especially for unsegmented languages, by providing the plugged-in resources including lexicon and corpus.

3 The proposed framework

In this paper, we focus on both language resources and the analysis modules as a complete framework for Thai-language intention and sentiment analysis. The proposed framework could easily be extended to support other languages by constructing language-specific resources. Our framework is also designed for easy adaptation to businesses in different domains. Similar to language-specific support, to apply the proposed framework for a specific domain, one can use the provided tagging tool to prepare domain-specific resources, i.e., annotated corpus and lexicon.

3.1 Components and modules

The proposed S-Sense framework (shown in Figure 1) consists of the following components.

- **Text collecting & processing**: This component involves the process of crawling and collecting social media contents from different websites. The process includes basic text processing, i.e., sentence segmentation, tokenization and normalization. Term normalization is the process of converting a word as appeared in the text into a predefined term and cleaning extra repeated characters which are not part of the term. For example, a word "thnxsss" can be normalized to the term "thank".

- **UREKA**: The main task of UREKA (Utilization on REsource for Knowledge Acquisition) is to extract key feature terms or phrases from a given text. Terms or phrases which are statistically significant in the corpus can be presented as interesting issues to the users. Another task is to filter and classify a given text into a topic. When collecting texts from social networking websites, it is very common to see many collected texts are not relevant to the brands or products being monitored. Therefore, a classification model could be trained to filter out the irrelevant texts from the corpus. After obtaining the relevant texts, another classification model could be trained to classify each text into a predefined set of topics. For example, in mobile service domain, topics could include signal quality, promotion and customer service.

- **S-Sense**: This is the main analysis component under the framework. S-Sense consists of four analysis modules. Language usage analysis classifies each text based on two aspects, the use of obscene language and the use of chat or informal languages. Detecting obscenity is useful since many texts with strongly negative sentiment could sometimes contain obscene language. Intention analysis classifies each text into four classes: *announcement*, *request*, *question* and *sentiment*. Sentiment analysis further classifies each text based on its sentiment, i.e., positive or negative. Emotion analysis is set in our future work. The task of emotion analysis module is to perform an in-depth sentiment analysis regarding to the emotion or feeling such as sad, happy and angry. Other components of S-Sense include visualizing modules including adaptive emoticon and interactive dashboard. These modules are used for displaying the summarized reports for the analyzed texts.

- **Tagging tool and language resources**: Under the proposed framework, language resources include two components, annotated corpus with domain and language-specific lexicons. To construct language resources, we provide a tagging tool for linguists to work with. The tagging tool is a web-based application which consists of a DBMS and a GUI.

3.2 Analysis tasks

The current version of S-Sense framework focuses on two main analysis modules, intention and sentiment. The intention analysis include the following categories.

1. **Announcement**: This type of intention refers to messages or posts in which a company intends to communicate with their customers, e.g., advertisement of new products or event announcement.

2. **Request**: This intention is used for customers to ask for help when having trouble or problem with the company's products or services.

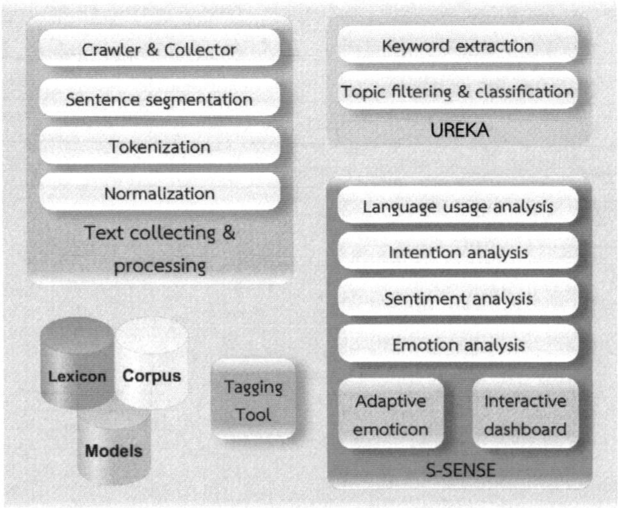

Figure 1: The proposed S-Sense framework.

Customers would expect immediate response from the company to solve the problem.

3. **Question**: This intention refers to messages or posts from customers asking for information related to products and services. The question is, for example, a customer's post asking for more details of a new mobile service promotion.

4. **Sentiment**: This intention is when customers express their opinions or sentiments towards the company's brand, products and services. Sentiment can be divided into positive, neutral and negative aspects.

It is important to analyze intention before performing sentiment analysis. Without intention analysis, a sentence containing positive polar words such as an advertisement would be identified as containing the sentiment intention. For example, a sentence "The new high-speed Internet is faster and cheaper. Apply today at the shop near you." is an advertisement, but could be incorrectly identified as having positive sentiment. Therefore, Identifying a sentence as announcement or advertisement would help improve overall performance of sentiment analysis.

3.3 Potential applications

S-Sense can be applied in many different applications. Some of the potential applications are as follows.

- **Brand monitoring**: With the widespread of social media, today customers have more freedom to express their sentiments towards products and services. Analyzing sentiments of the customers could help companies gain some insight on how they feel when using their products and services. More importantly, many companies are highly associated with their brands. Negative sentiments towards the company's brand could have negative impact on the product sales. Therefore, it is very important for companies to monitor or track the mentions and sentiments of the customers on social media.

- **Campaign Monitoring**: Many times throughout the year, the company would launch different campaigns involving new products and services. The goal of campaign monitoring (i.e, tracking) is to measure the customers' feedback on each campaign. The results could be analyzed in terms of number of mentions, positive and negative sentiments and the key product or service features in which customers feel positive or negative about.

- **Competitive Analysis**: This task is to monitor and analyze the activities including sentiments of customers towards the company's competitors. The analysis results could help gain some insight on strengths and weaknesses of the competitors in the market. For example, if a competitor has many complaints on certain product features, the company could grab the opportunity by advertising its own product features which are better than the competitor's.

- **Employee Engagement**: One of the main problems in many organizations today is the high turnover rate. One of the solutions is to monitor and analyze the employee engagement level. This task is to measure the employees' sentiments towards their jobs, colleagues and organization. The measure could reveal how much employees are willing to learn and perform at work, and to get involved in different activities initiated by the organization.

4 Experiments and discussion

To evaluate the proposed framework, we perform experiments using a corpus in the domain of mobile service. The corpus is obtained between March and June in 2013 from two sources, *Twitter*[3] and *Pantip*[4], one of the top visited web boards in Thailand. The total number of randomly selected texts in the corpus is *2,723*. The corpus was annotated in two aspects, intention and sentiment. Table 1 summarizes the number of tagged texts in four different intentions. The majority of intentions is sentiment which accounts for approximately 64% of the corpus. The reason is when using social networking websites or web boards, users often express their opinion and sentiment more than other intentions.

For the sentiment intention, we further annotated each text based on its sentiment, i.e., positive or negative. Table 2 summarizes the number of tagged texts in positive and negative sentiment. It can be observed that negative sentiment accounts for approximately 91%. This is not very surprising since users tend to complain when having problems using the mobile service. Major reported problems in mobile service industry include, for example, weak or unavailable signal, call drop, slow data transfer rate, impolite service and long waiting time for call center.

Table 3 shows some examples of annotated corpus in different intention and sentiment. In addition to annotating each text with an intention label,

[3]Twitter, *http://twitter.com*

[4]Pantip, *http://pantip.com*

Intention	# Texts
Announcement	94
Request	405
Question	456
Sentiment	1,768
Total	**2,723**

Table 1: Number of tagged texts in four different intentions.

Sentiment	# Texts
Positive	156
Negative	1,612
Total	**1,768**

Table 2: Number of tagged texts in positive and negative sentiments.

we collect clue terms which could help identify the intention. For example, from the announcement intention, the terms and phrases "new promotion", "best-deal" and "will start on" are collected into the clue lexicon. From the sentiment intention, we collected the terms "annoyed" and "impressive". Other clue terms are underlined for each example in the table.

Table 4 shows the statistics of lexicons used in the experiments. There are two types of lexicons: *general* and *clue* terms. General lexicon include two sets of terms, LEX*i*TRON[5] which are general words from Thai dictionary, and *Twitter* which contains newly found words from Thai Twitter corpus. Words obtained from Twitter include slangs and transliterated words from other languages. Clue lexicon include terms or phrases which could help identify intention and sentiment. One of the main objectives in the experiments is to observe the effect of incorporating clue lexicon in constructing classification models for intention and sentiment analysis. Therefore, we perform a comparative study on using different sets of lexicons.

To perform experiments, we apply the multinomial Naive Bayes algorithm to learn the classification models (McCallum and Nigam, 1998). The reason we use Naive Bayes is due to the small number of sample texts in the corpus, especially

[5]LEX*i*TRON, *http://lexitron.nectec.or.th*

Intention		Example
Announcement		อัตราค่าบริการ Happy Bonus ปรับปรุงใหม่จ๊ะ เริ่มใช้วันที่ 1 ค่ะ The new service fee for Happy Bonus will start on the 1st of this month.
		โปรใหม่!! ทรูมูฟ... ซิมสุดคุ้ม โปรวินาทีละ 1 ส.ต. ตลอด 24 ชั่วโมง New promotion!! True Move... Best-deal SIM, 1 satang / second all day and night.
Request		สมัครใช้บริการ Call Screening เองไม่ได้ CC ช่วยด้วยครับ I can't apply for Call Screening myself. CC (Call Center), please help me.
		รบกวนCC AISหน่อยค่ะ..เงินในโทรศัพท์หายไปไหนไม่รู้ (- -)?? AIS Call Center, please.. My pre-paid balance has gone missing without a clue ??
Question		โทรศัพท์หาย จะทำซิมใหม่เบอร์เดิมของ ais ต้องใช้เอกสารอะไรบ้างครับ I lost my phone. To get a new SIM card, what documents are required?
		โปรไหนของ one-2-call ที่รอรับสายได้นานสุดครับ Which promotion package of one-2-call allows the longest call waiting time?
Sentiment	Negative	น่ารำคาญมาก DTAC เมื่อไหร่จะปรับปรุงสัญญาณสักที โดยเฉพาะบนBTS Very annoyed. DTAC, when will you improve the signal? Especially on the BTS.
	Positive	ขอบคุณและชื่นชม เจ้าหน้าที่ AIS serenade call center ประทับใจครับ Thank you to the operator at AIS serenade call center. Very impressive.

Table 3: Example of annotated texts categorized by different intentions and sentiments.

Lexicon		# Terms
General	Lexitron	35,328
	Twitter	1,341
Clue	Announcement	86
	Request	177
	Question	454
	Polar (Negative)	1,675
	Polar (Positive)	1,237

Table 4: Two types of lexicons: *general* and *clue*

for the announcement intention. Naive Bayes only requires a small amount of training data to estimate the parameters for learning the models. Also Naive Bayes is a descriptive and probabilistic machine learning, therefore, the results could be easily analyzed and explained. The classification results are returned with a probability value which could be interpreted as the confidence level.

The first experiment is the intention analysis. For each intention listed in Table 1, we train a binary classification model with two classes, *related* and *other*. If a given text is analyzed as containing a particular intention, it will be assigned with the class label *related*. We prepare the data set by using the same amount of texts in each class. For example, in announcement intention, we use 94 announcement texts and randomly select another 94 texts from other intentions. To see the advantage of using clue terms as additional term feature, we compare the results between using only general lexicon and using both general and clue lexicons. The performance metric is *accuracy* which is defined as the number of correctly classified instances over the total number of test instances.

Table 5 shows the experimental results for intention analysis. The results are based on 10-fold cross validation. From the table, it can be observed that adding clue terms into the term feature helps improve the classification accuracy for all intentions. Especially for request, question and sentiment, the improvement is over 6%. For announcement, the improvement is approximately 2%. This is probably due to the difficulty in defining and collecting the clue terms for announcement intention. For example, some of the terms like "new" must be collocated with other term in a phrase, e.g. "new promotion". As the phrase becomes more specific, it will not be found in the test instances. Another observation is the request intention is the most difficult to analyze. This is due to often when users wish to request for something, there is no specific term or clue term in the message. The request intention is implicitly expressed with verbs or polar terms, therefore causing confusion to other intention classes.

Intention	Term feature	Accuracy (%)
Announcement	General	78.72
	General + Clue	**80.85**
Request	General	63.08
	General + Clue	**69.38**
Question	General	73.13
	General + Clue	**79.82**
Sentiment	General	67.47
	General + Clue	**73.61**

Table 5: Experimental results on intention analysis

The second experiment is the sentiment analysis. We train a binary classification model with two classes, *positive* and *negative*. The number of instances for each class is given in Table 2. Table 6 shows the experimental results on sentiment analysis. The results are based on 10-fold cross validation. From the table, we can observe that using clue terms as additional term features helps increase the accuracy by approximately 2%. The small amount in improvement is probably due to terms in general dictionary and from Twitter contain sentiment which already helps identify the polarity of the texts.

Term feature	Accuracy (%)
General	89.55
General + Clue	**91.64**

Table 6: Experimental results on sentiment analysis

To perform error analysis, we look at the test instances which are misclassified, i.e., classifying positive into negative and vice versa. We can summarize two major causes of errors as word sense ambiguity and sarcasm. The first problem occurs when a polar term contains both positive and negative senses depending on the contexts. For example, the word "strong", when appearing with the term "signal" will give positive polarity. However, when it appears with the term "employee", the term has the meaning of "impolite" and a negative polarity should be assigned. However, due to the small corpus size and simple feature vector which treats each term independent, sometimes, the terms cannot be learned properly. To solve this problem, we will explore the idea of incorporating contextual terms with the clue terms in our future work. Each clue term will be associated with some context terms to identify the polarity of the texts.

The second problem is sarcasm which is much more difficult to solve. This problem is still a difficult and challenging task in sentiment analysis of any languages (González-Ibáñez et al., 2004). While there are some research work to identify sarcasm in given texts, the performance is still poor. However, some of the sarcastic texts can still be identified by detecting some common slangs which are usually used in sarcastic texts. In Thai language, if users express a positive sentiment in an exaggerated way or in a contradicting way, then the message is most likely sarcastic. For example, "Today the download speed is faster than the speed of light. Thank you very much!" is considered as sarcastic.

5 Conclusion and future work

We proposed a framework called *S-Sense* (Social Media Sensing) for developing a social media analyzing tool. The current version focuses on intention and sentiment analysis. We applied the Naive Bayes as the classification algorithm to analyze four different intentions (announcement, request, question and sentiment) and two sentiments (positive and negative). The proposed framework was evaluated by using a social media corpus in the domain of mobile service obtained from *Twitter* and *Pantip* web board.

To study the effect of using different lexicon sets to train the models, we compared two approaches: using only general lexicon and using both general lexicon and clue terms. The results showed that adding clue terms into feature vector for training the classification models helps improve the accuracy for all intention and sentiment analysis models. For intention models of request, question and sentiment, the accuracy is increased by approximately 6%. For sentiment model, the accuracy is increased by approximately 2%.

From the error analysis, we found that two major problems are word sense ambiguity and sarcasm. For future work, we plan to improve the performance of both intention and sentiment analysis models by incorporating the contexts nearby the clue terms. Considering contexts could help reduce the disambiguation of the word sense. Another plan is to construct the lexicon and corpus for other different domains. In addition to mobile service, other business domains in Thailand often mentioned in the social media are automotive, consumer electronics, fashion, healthcare and tourism.

References

Philip Beineke, Trevor Hastie and Shivakumar Vaithyanathan. 2004. The sentimental factor: improving review classification via human-provided information. *Proc. of the 42nd Annual Meeting on Association for Computational Linguistics*, 263–270.

Xiaowen Ding, Bing Liu and Philip S. Yu. 2008. A holistic lexicon-based approach to opinion mining. *Proc. of the int. conf. on web search and web data mining*, 231–240.

Roberto González-Ibáñez, Smaranda Muresan and Nina Wacholder. 2011. Identifying sarcasm in Twitter: a closer look. *Proc. of the 49th ACL: Human Language Technologies*, 581–586.

Choochart Haruechaiyasak, Alisa Kongthon, Pornpimon Palingoon, Chatchawal Sangkeettrakarn. 2010. Constructing Thai Opinion Mining Resource: A Case Study on Hotel Reviews. *Proc. of the Eighth Workshop on Asian Language Resources*, 64–71.

Minqing Hu and Bing Liu. 2004. Mining and summarizing customer reviews. *Proc. of the 10th ACM SIGKDD international conference on Knowledge discovery and data mining*, 168–177.

Wei Jin, Hung Hay Ho and Rohini K. Srihari. 2009. OpinionMiner: a novel machine learning system for web opinion mining and extraction. *Proc. of the 15th ACM SIGKDD*, 1195–1204.

Soo-Min Kim and Eduard Hovy. 2004. Determining the sentiment of opinions. *Proc. of the 20th international conference on Computational Linguistics*, 1367–1373.

Lun-Wei Ku and Hsin-Hsi Chen. 2007 Mining opinions from the Web: Beyond relevance retrieval. *Journal of American Society for Information Science and Technology*, 58(12):1838–1850.

Lun-Wei Ku, Ting-Hao Huang and Hsin-Hsi Chen. 2009. Using morphological and syntactic structures for Chinese opinion analysis. *Proc. of the 2009 empirical methods in natural language processing*, 1260–1269.

Andrew McCallum and Kamal Nigam. 1998. A Comparison of Event Models for Naive Bayes Text Classification. *Proc. of the AAAI-98 Workshop on 'Learning for Text Categorization'* 41–48.

Bo Pang, Lillian Lee and Shivakumar Vaithyanathan. 2002. Thumbs up?: sentiment classification using machine learning techniques. *Proc. of the ACL-02 conf. on empirical methods in natural language processing*, 79–86.

Mikalai Tsytsarau and Themis Palpanas. 2012. Survey on mining subjective data on the web. *Data Mining and Knowledge Discovery*, 24(3): 478–514.

Theresa Wilson, Janyce Wiebe and Paul Hoffmann. 2009. Recognizing contextual polarity: An exploration of features for phrase-level sentiment analysis. *Comput. Linguist.*, 35(3):399–433.

Social Metaphor Detection via Topical Analysis

Ting-Hao (Kenneth) Huang
Language Technologies Institute, Carnegie Mellon University
5000 Forbes Ave., Pittsburgh, PA 15213, USA
windx@cmu.edu

Abstract

With massive social media data, e.g., comments, blog articles, or tweets, become available, there is a rising interest towards automatic metaphor detection from open social text. One of the most well-known approaches is detecting the violation of selectional preference. The idea of selectional preference is that verbs tend to have semantic preferences of their arguments. If we find that in some text, any arguments of these predicates are not of their preferred semantic classes, and it's very likely to be a metaphor. However, previously only few papers have focuses on leveraging topical analysis techniques in metaphor detection. Intuitively, both predicates and arguments exhibit strong tendencies towards a few specific topics, and this topical information provides additional evidence to facilitate identification of selectional preference among text. In this paper, we study how the metaphor detection technique can be influenced by topical analysis techniques based on our proposed three-step approach. We formally define the problem, and propose our approach for metaphor detection, and then we conduct experiments on a real-world data set. Though our experimental result shows that topics do not have strong impacts on the metaphor detection techniques, we analyze the result and present some insights based on our study.

1 Introduction

With massive social media data, e.g., comments, blog articles, or tweets, become available, there is a rising interest towards automatic metaphor detection from open social text. One of the most well-known approaches is detecting the violation of selectional preference. The idea of selectional preference is that the predicates (mostly verbs) tend to have semantic preferences of their arguments. For instance, the verb "flex" has a strong preference of "muscle" and "bone" as its object. If we find that in some text, the object of "flex" is not of the semantic class of "muscle" and "bone", it's very likely to be a metaphorical use.

Previously, researchers have studies metaphor identification by modeling selectional preference (Loenneker-Rodman and Narayanan, 2010; Shutova *et al.*, 2010; Shutova, 2010; Resnik, 1997; Shutova and Teufel, 2010; Calzolari *et al.*, 2010; Preiss *et al.*, 2007), while only few papers have focused on leveraging topical analysis techniques in metaphor detection. The intuition behind combining metaphor identification and topic analysis is that both verbs and arguments exhibit strong tendencies towards a few specific topics, and this topical information provides additional evidence to facilitate identification of selectional preference among text. For instance, in the topic of sport, the subjects of "flex" are mostly humans; but in the topic of finance or politics, the subjects of "flex" are mostly organizations or countries, e.g., "*China to flex its financial muscles at US meeting.*" In this paper, we aim to study how the metaphor detection technique can be influenced based on topical analysis techniques.

The problem of automatic social metaphor detection via topical analysis poses several challenges:

First, as social media data is usually noisy, how to effectively preprocess the input texts before an actual detection component is employed should be carefully studied. We should empirically estimate the performance of existing NLP tools, especially lemmatizers and POS taggers.

Second, how we can automatically discover the topical distribution for each term (including verbs and nouns) within open text is not a trivial problem. Moreover, we also need to study how to leverage topical distribution of each verb and noun to metaphor detection.

Finally, how to apply and evaluate the proposed approach on a real world data set is not straight-forward, as there is hardly existing data set nor benchmark to evaluate metaphor detection, we need to create a benchmark that can effectively show that the performance difference.

In this paper, we formally define the problem, and propose our 3-step approach for metaphor

IJCNLP 2013 Workshop on Natural Language Processing for Social Media (SocialNLP), pages 14–22,
Nagoya, Japan, 14 October 2013.

detection, specifically, we first preprocess the input text by extracting tokens and further clustering nouns, and then we detect selectional association outlier, finally, we apply a selectional preference strength filter to extract metaphor-embedded text snippets.

We then conduct experiments on a real-world social media data set. The LDA model is applied to partition the input corpus based on topics, and we adopt the 3-step approach both on the whole corpus and every single topic data partitions, respectively. Finally, we compare the metaphor detection results between that with and without influences of topics, and to observe which one performs better.

The rest of the paper is organized as follows: In Section 2, we briefly summarize related work for metaphor detection based on selectional preference detection. In Section 3, we formally define the problem of automatic social metaphor detection. Then, in Section 4, we first conduct a preliminary test to compare two technologies for metaphor detection, and choose one to establish the 3-step framework describe in Section 5. In Section 6, we further discuss the details of topic analysis. Finally, we demonstrate the experiment in Section 7, discuss the results in Section 8, and conclude the whole work in Section 9.

2 Related Work

In this section, we briefly survey papers that investigate approaches to detect metaphor in text.

2.1 Automatic metaphor detection

There have been many computational approaches in the field of natural language processing toward modeling metaphors. Based on (Shutova *et al.*, 2010), the research of modeling metaphors could be divided into two sub-fields: metaphor detection and metaphor interpretation. In this paper, we focus on metaphor detection and aim to explore some new potential directions of this field.

Speaking of metaphor detection, the first challenge is how to define a metaphor. As mentioned in (Loenneker-Rodman and Narayanan, 2010), "*there is rich continuing theoretical debate on the definition and use of metaphor.*" In our work, we limited the scope of our research that we only aim to detect "non-conventionalized metaphor" which usually has low frequency and could reasonably be considered as outliers.

The Met* System (Fass, 1991) can be considered as the first attempt to explore this field, and the following approaches include (Goatly, 1997), (Peters and Peters, 2000), CorMet System (Mason, 2004), and TroFi System (Birke and Sarkar, 2006). Most of them adopt the concept of selectional preference which we mentioned above, along with some hand-coded knowledge base, e.g., VerbNet. VerbNet has the information about the constraint of arguments of verbs. By matching the text with verb and its argument, we're able to detect the violation of arguments. However, in this paper, we apply a different approach that learns the violations purely from statistics based on natural texts. One advantage of this method is that we don't need any hand-coded knowledge, so could be easier to be ported to other languages.

2.2 Topical analysis

Many topical analysis techniques have been developed, e.g., latent semantic analysis, probabilistic LSA, NMF, LDA, etc.

Latent Dirichlet Allocation (LDA) (Blei, Ng, and Jordan, 2003) models documents using a latent topic layer. In LDA, for each document d, a multinomial distribution θ_d over topics is first sampled from a Dirichlet distribution with parameter α. Second, for each word w_{di}, a topic z_{di} is chosen from this topic distribution. Finally, the word w_{di} is generated from a topic-specific multinomial distribution φ_{zdi}. Accordingly, the generating probability of word w from document d is:

$$P(w|d,\theta,\phi) = \sum_{z\in T} P(w|z,\phi_z)P(z|d,\theta_d)$$

Basically, we will use this approach as our topical analysis component to discover underlying topic distribution for nouns, verbs, and adjectives.

3 Problem Definition

In this section, we formally define the problem of the social metaphor detection via topic diversity identification.

Social Metaphor detection: We aim to recognize the non-conventionalized metaphors in social media text by a fully automatic approach, where the input would be real text from social media. Based on the word distribution among the input data, we aim to detect metaphors without using any external knowledge resources.

There are many sub-categories of metaphors. In this work, we only focus on "non-conventionalized metaphors", which could be reasonably considered as an outlier of language behavior. One advantage of non-conventionalized metaphors is that the approach can be language independent and need no external knowledge resource. This kind of framework could be simply ported to various languages.

We will present how to tackle the problem by our proposed 3-step framework and discuss how to take the advantage of topical analysis for metaphor detection. We will also show how to quantitatively calculate these values in next section.

4 Preliminary Test

As mentioned above, one of the most important approaches of metaphor detection is to detect the violation of selectional preference. However, none of other approaches are proposed as a baseline model to compare with it. In this section, to investigate the reliability of selectional preference modeling, we adopted another possible approach for metaphor detection, i.e., the semantic outlier word detection, and ran a preliminary test to compare their performance.

4.1 Semantic Outlier Word Detection

Intuitively, for a certain topic, people tend to use the words that are "semantically more related" to the topic. Therefore, we can estimate that the set of words which are usually used to describe a certain topic are more strongly related to each other than to the words used to describe other topics. For instance, the words used to describe "finance", e.g., bank, money, business, are semantically more similar (or related) to each other than to the words used to describe "entertainment", e.g., movie, music, star, etc. Based on this idea, we can detect the "semantic outlier" in a chunk of text, which can indicate the words that are borrowed from other topics to establish metaphors.

In this paper, we basically followed the method proposed by (Inkpen and Désilets, 2005) to detect the semantic outlier words. For one input sentence, we first use the DISCO[1] package to calculate the pair-wise semantic similarities between any two words within the sentence, and then calculate the average of three greatest similarities of each word as its "semantic coherence (SC)." Finally, the semantic outliers tend to have obviously lower semantic coherence than other words, so we just set an empirical threshold to capture those outliers.

[1] http://www.linguatools.de/

4.2 Selectional Association Outlier Detection

Selectional preference (also referred to as selectional association or selectional restriction) describes the semantic preference of predicates to noun classes in a given grammatical relation. For instance, the predicate "eat" prefers the noun class of "food" as its *direct object* more than the noun class "building", and also prefers the noun class of "human" and "animal" as its *subject* more than the noun class "vehicle". Modeling selectional preference could help us to find the anomaly grammatical argument, which is an important clue of metaphorical languages.

In this paper, for a given predicate *p* and a semantic noun class *c*, we adopt the measure of selectional association (SA), which is proposed by (Resnik, 1997), to present the selectional preference value between them. Selectional association equation can be calculated similar to point-wise mutual information, as follows,

$$A_R(p,c) = \frac{1}{S_R(p)} \Pr(c|p) \log \frac{\Pr(c|p)}{\Pr(c)}$$

A_R is the selectional association value between a given predicate *p* and a semantic noun class *c*. S_R is the selectional preference strength of *p*, which can be formally defined similar to the K-L divergence between prior and posterior, as follows:

$$S_R(p,c) = D(\Pr(c|p)||\Pr(c)) = \sum_c \Pr(c|p) \log \frac{\Pr(c|p)}{\Pr(c)}$$

Finally, similar as the Section 4.1, the selectional preference outliers tend to have obviously lower SA value than others, so we just set an empirical threshold to capture those outliers. Note that for this preliminary test, we only focus on the direct-object (*dobj*) and subject (*subj*) grammatical relations.

4.3 Experiment and Discussion

Since labeling metaphor embedded sentences are effort consuming, we conduct experiment on a benchmark corpus, which contains 122 sentences extracted from the Web, where 61 (50%) of them contain metaphor, and 61 of them don't contain metaphor.

We apply both approaches on this data set. For the selectional association outlier detection, the best resulting F-1 score is 0.58 with precision of 0.60, and recall of 0.56. On the other hand, for the semantic outlier word detection, regardless of which value of threshold we set, the performance remains very low. This method returns huge amount of false positive semantic outliers. Mainly due to two reasons: First, the semantic coherence can be easily affected by very general words, which usually have very high similarities and also occur very often. If one sentence has more than one very general context words, e.g., "take", "put", or "get", the semantic coherences of all other words could be systematically increased, and thus fail to represent the outlier words. We believe that's the main reason why this method can not detect the semantic outlier we expected. Second, the measure of semantic similarity between word pairs is not very reliable for low frequency words. The similarities calculations which are based on the text of big corpus usually have this problem: It's reliable on high frequency words, but not on low frequency words, which exactly are what we aim to capture.

To conclude, the selectional association outlier detection method obviously outperform the semantic outlier word detection in the preliminary test. Therefore, in this paper, we only focus on selectional association to develop our technology.

5 3-Step Framework of Metaphor Detection

In this section, we introduce our approach to the problem of social metaphor detection.

In particular, our approach consists of three steps: (1) word extraction and building noun clustering, (2) selectional association outlier detection, (3) selectional preference strength filter. The first step deals with noisy input social media data, and produce relatively clean output with richer NLP information labeled on the text, and in the second step, we use statistical method to calculate the selectional association scores of particular types of token pairs based on the tokens and noun clusters extracted from the first step. Finally, as a post-process step, the output generated from the first step will be further analyzed and filtered out false positives based on empirical threshold.

5.1 Step 1: Word extraction and noun clustering

Different from well phased corpora, e.g., Wall Street Journal, or Wikipedia pages, that are used by other metaphor detection methods, social metaphors tend to be embedded in noisy social media text, e.g., blog and forum texts. The goal of word extraction is to filter out the noise from grammatically structured phrases and tokens.

We first use a POS tagger to label the tokens with part-of-speech tags. However, since the POS taggers unlikely produce high quality results on noisy data. We only select nouns with word frequency greater than 5, and greater than 70% of the overall occurrences as a noun. For adjectives and verbs, more strictly, we require the word frequency greater than 50, and over 80% of all occurrences should be adjectives or verbs.

Then based on the nouns we extracted, we build a set of semantic noun clusters, which is the foundation for modeling the selectional preference. In this work, we apply spectral clustering algorithm. Specifically,

1. For each noun, we use the DICSO toolkit to extract their top 100 semantically similar nouns (from Wikipedia). For the first similar words, the similarity weight is set to 1/2; the second is 1/3, the third is 1/4, and so on.
2. We use this information as feature, and run the spectral clustering algorithm among all nouns we extracted.

Note that though the DISCO toolkit calculates word similarity based on Wikipedia, which is a reliable corpus, we only focus on the nouns actually occur in the input data set, i.e., the social media data. Namely, if a certain noun appears in the extracted "top 100 semantically similar nouns" but never occurs in the input data, we just ignore it.

5.2 Step 2: Selectional association outlier detection

Based on the formula mentioned in the Section 4.2 and the semantic noun clusters built in Step 1, we measure the selctional associations for the most frequent verbs we extracted, particularly on the three kinds of grammatical relations, namely, adjective modifier (*amod*), direct object (*dobj*), and subject (*subj*).

In this work, we intentionally include the adjective modifier relation. When speaking of the selectional preference, most previous work focus only on verbal predicates. However, in the grammatical relation of adjective modifier, the modifier can also be considered as a predicate, and the modifyees are mostly also nouns. Therefore, we also aim to apply our approach on the *amod* relation, and see if the method also effectively captures adjective metaphors.

We considered the relations with negative SA values as "SA outliers", and thus labeled the sentences containing "SA outliers" as metaphors.

5.3 Step 3: Selectional preference strength filter

As mentioned in the Section 4.3, selectional preference strength of a predicate is defined as the K-L divergence between the prior and the posterior of noun clusters. For the predicates with strong preference, e.g., "filmmake", it significantly affect the posterior probability distribution of noun clusters. In the case of the direct object of "filmmake", the probability of "movie/film" noun class is hugely increased. On the other hand, some light verb, e.g., "get", "put", "take", have quite weak preferences toward their direct object or subject.

The idea of selectional preference filter is first proposed by (Shutova, *et al.*, 2010), which suggests that the predicates with less strong selectional preference would barely "violates" their own weak preference. Therefore, if we filter out the predicates with weak selectional preference, the false positives of metaphor detection will be reduced, and the precision will significantly increase. In our framework, we apply this filter as the final step. Note that due to the lack of training and developing data, we just set the same threshold, which is 1.32, as suggested as that in (Shutova, *et al.*, 2010).

6 Topic Model Analysis

We use LDA to model the topical distribution of words and documents of corpora, and we want to observe the changes of selectional preferences among various topics. The steps are as follows,

1. We train an LDA topic model with *k* various topics based on the whole input data set, i.e., social media corpus.
2. For each document *d* in the input data set, we assign *d* to its favorite topic. Namely, we partition the corpus into *k* document collections based on topics.
3. Run the 3-step process mentioned in the Section 5 on the whole data set, and also on the *k* different document collections, respectively.
4. Compare the SA outlier detection results among the data with and without topic modeling.

The underlying hypothesis in this comparison is that the selectional preference would increase for certain predicates in certain topics, and thus the outlier of SA values would be further emphasized. In that case, the metaphor detection technique could be improved.

7 Experiment

7.1 Data and Setting

Our method requires the fully-parsed data set, so we decide to choose a reasonable size of social media data. We collected the whole text of posts from a large online breast cancer support community which is also used in (Wen, *et al.*, 2013), and then parse it by the Stanford Parser toolkit[2]. In our word extraction step, we extract 55,511 distinct nouns, 3,242 distinct adjectives, and 1,827 distinct verbs.

Note that in the noun clustering step, we manually removed the following 3 clusters to avoid some systematic parsing errors of the Stanford parser:

- *hours, minutes, times, days, weeks, months, seconds, ...*
- *yourselves, oneself, somebody, everybody, someone, anything, everything, anyone, ...*
- *boy, girl, child, woman, children, guy, kid, person, ...*

In the topic model analysis phase, we adopt the JGibbLDA[3] toolkit to build the model, and set the number of topics (*k*) as 20.

7.2 Results and Case Study

For the whole data set, the top 10 sample detected selectional association outliers[4] (of the three grammatical relationships) are listed in the Table 1. We also demonstrate the result of one out of twenty topic document collections in the Table 2 for comparison. Note that example usages are lightly disguised based on the techniques suggested by (Bruckman, 2006).

[2] http://nlp.stanford.edu/software/lex-parser.shtml
[3] A Java Implementation of Latent Dirichlet Allocation (LDA) using Gibbs Sampling for Parameter Estimation and Inference:
http://jgibblda.sourceforge.net/
[4] For each pair of predicate and noun cluster, we try to select the most "metaphor-like" usage if multiple outliers are detected. To protect the privacy of forum users, we also skip all the examples which contain name entities.

Relation(arg0, arg1)	SA(10^{-3})	Example Usage	Analysis
amod			
amod(breast, yearly)	-2.7306	"yearly breast MRI"	Parsing Error
amod(skin, circular)	-2.7079	"circular skin patches"	Non-metaphor
amod(skin, greasy)	-2.6896	"greasy skin"	Non-metaphor
amod(head, administrative)	-2.6864	"the administrative head of this institute"	Weak metaphor
amod(hug, weary)	-2.6461	"…get weary. Hugs to you all…"	Sentence Segmentation Error
amod(breast, uncertain)	-2.6138	"The breast dimpling and uncertain mammography…"	Parsing Error
amod(kiss, french)	-2.5970	"…about French kiss…"	Non-metaphor
amod(breast, slim)	-2.5752	"My breasts are not slim but not fat..."	Non-metaphor
amod(tomorrow, crisp)	-2.5636	"…it's expected to be a crisp 72 tomorrow."	Parsing Error
amod(wing, seasoned)	-2.5510	"seasoned chicken wings"	Non-metaphor
dobj			
dobj(defy, breast)	-2.5893	"gravity defying breasts"	Parsing Error
dobj(occupy, breast)	-2.5749	"…(cancer) occupy the whole breast…"	Non-metaphor
dobj(sprinkle, germ)	-2.5350	"sprinkle wheat germ"	Non-metaphor
dobj(ooze, skin)	-2.5260	"oozing skin"	Non-metaphor
dobj(circulate, breast)	-2.5157	"…let air circulates around patient's breast."	Parsing Error
dobj(win, tomorrow)	-2.5095	"If John win tomorrow night, …"	Metonymy
dobj(hire, dvd)	-2.4972	"hire the dvd"	Non-metaphor
dobj(defy, cancer)	-2.4773	"…to defy the cancer and smile…"	Non-metaphor
dobj(float, cancer)	-2.4380	"…cancer cells float around in my blood…"	Non-metaphor
dobj(shut, head)	-2.4141	"…shut my head off…"	Metaphor
nsubj			
nsubj(cleanse, breast)	-2.5783	"breast cleanse"	Parsing Error
nsubj(metabolize, tumor)	-2.5513	"Tumors metabolize …"	Non-metaphor
nsubj(deny, adjuster)	-2.4950	"The claims adjuster denied this claim …"	Non-metaphor
nsubj(occupy, head)	-2.4827	"…keep my head occupied …"	Weak metaphor
nsubj(multiply, hug)	-2.4617	"…the hugs will multiply."	Metaphor
nsubj(constipate, hug)	-2.4286	"… hugs … that percocet is constipating."	Parsing Error
nsubj(overtake, belly)	-2.3276	"… my belly has overtaken the boobs …"	Metaphor
nsubj(multiply, treatment)	-2.2361	"…treatment for.. , multiply that by…"	Weak metaphor
nsubj(pay, patient)	-2.2164	"…patients pay for…"	Non-metaphor
nsubj(manufacture, expander)	-2.2056	"…ask the expander manufactures come up with better tissue expander."	Parsing Error

Table 1: Examples of Selectional Association Violation Identified without Topical Analysis

Relation(arg0, arg1)	SA(10^{-3})	Example Usage	Analysis
amod			
amod(head, gray)	-2.5469	"gray head"	Metonymy
amod(belly, former)	-2.5462	"your former belly"	Non-metaphor
amod(carcinoma, vaginal)	-2.5452	"… vaginal squamous cell carcinomas …"	Non-metaphor
amod(cancer, unilateral)	-2.5144	"unilateral breast cancer"	Non-metaphor
amod(breast, unilateral)	-2.4714	"unilateral breast"	Non-metaphor
amod(lesion, bilateral)	-2.3713	"bilateral lesions"	Non-metaphor
amod(treatment, immediate)	-2.3687	"immediate treatment"	Non-metaphor
amod(flyer, weekly)	-2.3064	"weekly flyer"	Non-metaphor
amod(symptom, bilateral)	-2.2976	"bilateral symptoms"	Non-metaphor
amod(tumor, enlarged)	-2.2626	"enlarged malignant tumor"	Non-metaphor
dobj			
dobj(celebrate, cancer)	-2.7801	"…celebrate my 10th cancer free year."	Parsing Error
dobj(weigh, head)	-2.7256	"So many questions … is weighing my head."	Metaphor
dobj(join, skin)	-2.7097	"…join the skin together…"	Non-metaphor
dobj(draw, nose)	-2.4197	"…drew a nose on it."	Non-metaphor
dobj(play, cheek)	-2.3255	"…play up my eyes…"	Non-metaphor
dobj(join, slew)	-2.1792	"Mary joined a slew of women …"	Non-metaphor
dobj(play, tomorrow)	-2.1190	"Playing golf tomorrow…"	Parsing Error
dobj(apply, forehead)	-2.0029	"…apply directly to the forehead."	Non-metaphor
dobj(pay, cancer)	-1.9471	"…price to pay for surviving cancer…"	Non-metaphor
dobj(regain, head)	-1.9457	"…regained a full head of hair…"	Parsing Error
nsubj			
nsubj(specialize, patient)	-2.3001	"…specializes in working with breast cancer patients, …"	Parsing Error
nsubj(pay, treatment)	-2.2237	"…get the treatment and self pay, …"	Parsing Error
nsubj(cover, cheek)	-2.0421	"…my cheeks covered with…"	Non-metaphor
nsubj(pay, head)	-1.8908	"…you're drinking safe and only your head is paying the price."	(Weak) metaphor
nsubj(pay, homeschooling)	-1.7228	"…the homeschooling paid off."	Non-metaphor
nsubj(build, expander)	-1.3925	"... an expander to build ..."	Parsing Error
nsubj(cover, melatonin)	-1.3865	"…melatonin covers the need for…"	Non-metaphor
nsubj(cover, wife)	-1.2500	"…so his wife should be covered…"	Non-metaphor
nsubj(cover, nurse)	-1.1849	"…the nurses talking about the insurance would cover it."	Parsing Error
nsubj(cover, dose)	-1.1708	"…do the single big dose to cover 2 weeks…"	Non-metaphor

Table 2: Examples of Selectional Association Violation Identified Based on Topical Analysis (for one Particular Topic)

We found that the strength of selectional preference of each predicates are actually increased in split topics. However, the increase has no clear benefits to metaphor detection in our result. It successfully detects "outliers", but those outliers are not necessarily to be metaphors.

Take the result of direct object for example. Without topic analysis, the top outliers we detected are (accomplish, Bianca), (defy, breast), (occupy, breast), (sprinkle, germ). Most of them are just rarely used verb-object combinations, but not metaphors. With topic analysis, we picked one topic out of twenty as example, the top outliers we detected are (celebrate, cancer), (join, skin), (draw, brow), (play, head). We can observe that the verbs and nouns are actually more concentrated. In this case, the topic seems like celebration/play/event/play. However, those pairs are also only rare, but not metaphors.

8 Discussion

Though the final result is not very promising, we gain some valuable experiences in this work.

Firstly, parsing error is lethal for our approach. It would hurt our performance in at least two aspects. Parsing errors would put incorrect nouns in the noun cluster, which is the foundation of the whole method. Furthermore, it would also create significant amount of noise in the data, and thus affect the statistical modeling phase. Therefore, the pre-processing is critical. After we added the strict word extraction strategy into our system, the quality of outputs is significantly improved.

Secondly, from our experiments, we found that the strength of selectional preference is actually increased when clustering the documents by topic modeling. In each topic's document collection, we collect documents by word co-occurrences. Therefore, predicates are more concentrated on their preferred grammatical arguments. However, the enhancement of selectional preference strength turned out not strong enough to improve metaphor detection. For some certain topic, the top SA outliers are even worse than that of the whole set, because selectional association is a linguistic phenomenon with high data sparsity. Partitioning would further reduce the amount of data, and affect the reliability of the model.

Finally, we also noticed that our fundamental hypothesis might not be accurate. We found that the SA outliers are not necessarily metaphors. Some of the outliers just rarely-used languages, or some "weird" usage, e.g., (hug, multiply) in "*the hugs we are storing will multiply*" of the Table 1, or the (play, head) in "*It keeps playing through my head now.*" of the Table 2. We might need to reconsider about the hypothesis we adopt in the future.

9 Conclusion and Future Work

In this paper, we try to leverage one of the most well-known approaches in detecting the violation of selectional preference with topical analysis techniques. The idea of selectional preference is that verbs tend to have semantic preferences of their arguments, while topical information provides additional evidence to facilitate identification of selectional preference among text. Though our experimental result shows that topics do not have strong impacts on the metaphor detection techniques, we analyze the result and present some insights based on our study.

As our next step, for reconsidering our hypothesis, we need to quantitatively compare our results on the gold-standard benchmark. Another interesting experiment might be to cluster the predicates, similar to nouns, as in our experiments, the predicates still suffer from sparsity issue.

Acknowledgments

Supported by the Intelligence Advanced Research Projects Activity (IARPA) via Department of Defense US Army Research Laboratory contract number W911NF-12-C-0020. The U.S. Government is authorized to reproduce and distribute reprints for Governmental purposes notwithstanding any copyright annotation thereon. Disclaimer: The views and conclusions contained herein are those of the authors and should not be interpreted as necessarily representing the official policies or endorsements, either expressed or implied, of IARPA, DoD/ARL, or the U.S. Government.

We would also like to thank Zi Yang for his help of the topical analysis experiments, Teruko Mitamura and Eric Nyberg for their instructions, and Yi-Chia Wang and Dong Nguyen for the work of data collection.

References

Birke, J., and Sarkar, A. 2006. A clustering approach for the nearly unsupervised recognition of nonliteral language. In Proceedings of EACL, volume 6, 329–336.

Blei, D.; Ng, A.; and Jordan, M. 2003. Latent dirichlet allocation. the Journal of machine Learning research 3:993–1022.

Bruckman, Amy. (2006). Teaching students to study online communities ethically. Journal of Information Ethics, 15(2), 82-98.

Calzolari, N.; Choukri, K.;Maegaard, B.;Mariani, J.; Odijk, J.; Piperidis, S.; Rosner, M.; and Tapias, D., eds. 2010. Proceedings of the International Conference on Language Resources and Evaluation, LREC 2010, 17-23 May 2010, Valletta, Malta. European Language Resources Association.

Fass, D. 1991. met*: A method for discriminating metonymy and metaphor by computer. Computational Linguistics 17(1):49–90.

Goatly, A. 1997. The language of metaphors, volume 3. Routledge London.

Inkpen, D., and Désilets, A. 2005. Semantic similarity for detecting recognition errors in automatic speech transcripts.

Loenneker-Rodman, B., and Narayanan, S. 2010. Computational approaches to figurative language. Cambridge Encyclopedia of Psycholinguistics.

Mason, Z. 2004. Cormet: a computational, corpus-based conventional metaphor extraction system. Computational Linguistics 30(1):23–44.

Ng, A.; Jordan, M.; Weiss, Y.; *et al.* 2002. On spectral clustering: Analysis and an algorithm. Advances in neural information processing systems 2:849–856.

Peters,W., and Peters, I. 2000. Lexicalised systematic polysemy in wordnet. In Proc. Secondt Intnl Conf on Language Resources and Evaluation.

Preiss, J.; Briscoe, T.; and Korhonen, A. 2007. A system for large-scale acquisition of verbal, nominal and adjectival subcategorization frames from corpora. In ANNUAL MEETING-ASSOCIATION FOR COMPUTATIONAL LINGUISTICS, volume 45, 912.

Resnik, P. 1997. Selectional preference and sense disambiguation. In Proceedings of the ACL SIGLEX Workshop on Tagging Text with Lexical Semantics: Why, What, and How, 52–57. Washington, DC.

Shutova, E., and Teufel, S. 2010. Metaphor corpus annotated for source-target domain mappings. In Proceedings of LREC.

Shutova, E.; Sun, L.; and Korhonen, A. 2010. Metaphor identification using verb and noun clustering. In Proceedings of the 23rd International Conference on Computational Linguistics, 1002–1010. Association for Computational Linguistics.

Shutova, E. 2010. Models of metaphor in nlp. In Proceedings of the 48th Annual Meeting of the Association for Computational Linguistics, 688–697. Association for Computational Linguistics.

Wen, M., Zheng, Z., Jang, H., Xiang, G., and Rose, C. (2013). Extracting Events with Informal Temporal References in Personal Histories in Online Communities. ACL'13.

The New Eye of Government: Citizen Sentiment Analysis in Social Media

Ravi Arunachalam
IBM
rarunach@in.ibm.com

Sandipan Sarkar
IBM
sandipansarkar@gmail.com,
sandipan.sarkar@in.ibm.com

Abstract

Several Governments across the world are trying to move closer to their citizens to achieve transparency and engagement. The explosion of social media is opening new opportunities to achieve it. In this work we proposed an approach to monitor and analyze the citizen sentiment in social media by Governments. We also applied this approach to a real-world problem and presented how Government agencies can get benefited out of it.

1 Introduction

Governments across the world facing unique challenges today than ever before. In recent time, *Arab Spring* phenomenon is an example of how Governments can be impacted if they ignore citizen sentiment. It is a growing trend that Governments are trying to move closer to the citizen-centric model, where the priorities and services would be driven according to citizen needs rather than Government capability. Such trends are forcing the Governments in rethinking and reshaping their policies in citizen interactions. New disruptive technologies like cloud, mobile etc. are opening new opportunities to the Governments to enable innovations in such interactions.

The advent of Social Media is a recent addition to such disruptive socio-technical enablers. Governments are fast realizing that it can be a great vehicle to get closer to the citizens. It can provide deep insight in what citizens want. Thus, in the current gloomy climate of world economy today, Governments can reorganize and reprioritize the allocation limited funds, thereby creating maximum impact on citizens' life. Building such insight is a non-trivial task because of the huge volume of information that social media can generate. However, Sentiment Analysis or Opinion Mining can be a useful vehicle in this journey.

In this work, we presented a model and case study to analyze citizen sentiment from social media in helping the Governments to take decisions.

2 Background

2.1 Social Sentiment Analysis

The social media is transforming the way we communicate, the way we form relationships, the way we connect to each other, the way we live and work. Here are some figures that give an idea about the frantic pace in which the social media phenomenon is growing: 1.43 billion people worldwide visited a social networking site in 2012[1]; nearly 1 in 8 people worldwide have their own Facebook page[2]; 3 million new blogs come online every month[3]; and 65 percent of social media users said they use it to learn more about brands, products and services[4].

Mass Communication expert Curtis (2013) divided the history of social media into three phases – *Before the Dawn* (1969 - 1993), *The Dawning* (1994 - 2004) and *After the Dawn* (2005 onwards). The works on social sentiment analysis has started to be reported after the last phase commenced, when the social media has received its maturity.

Around 2007, the researchers and analysts started to take notice of the importance and value of social media monitoring and sentiment analysis as a means to achieve it. An Aberdeen Group

---

[1] http://searchenginewatch.com/article/2167518/Worldwide-Social-Media-Usage-Trends-in-2012 (Accessed on 6 Jun 2013)
[2] http://ignitevisibility.com/facebook-marketing/ (Accessed on 6 Jun 2013)
[3] http://www.jeffbullas.com/2012/11/28/the-latest-27-social-media-facts-figures-and-statistics-for-2012-infographic/ (Accessed on 6 Jun 2013)
[4] http://www.nielsen.com/us/en/reports/2012/state-of-the-media-the-social-media-report-2012.html (Accessed on 6 Jun 2013)

IJCNLP 2013 Workshop on Natural Language Processing for Social Media (SocialNLP), pages 23–28,
Nagoya, Japan, 14 October 2013.

Benchmark Report (Zabin and Jefferies, 2008) published around same time showed that more than 84% best-in-class companies improved their overall performance, customer satisfaction, risk management and actionable insights from social media monitoring and analysis.

We found the first publication on social sentiment analysis in a most interesting paper by Abbasi (2007), where he proposed an affect analysis approach for measuring the presence of hate, violence, and the resulting propaganda dissemination across extremist group forums. In a similar application, Bermingham et al. (2009) proposed crawling and analyzing social media sites, such as YouTube, to detect radicalism. Martineau and Finin (2009) proposed Delta TFIDF, a new technique to efficiently weight words before classification. Asur and Huberman (2010) proposed an approach to predict real-world outcomes through social media sentiment analysis. Pak and Paroubek (2010) explored the use of Twitter as a corpus for sentiment analysis. Bollen et al. (2011) went ahead and analyzed Twitter content to detect different moods of the microbloggers and linked that with the major events in market, media and culture in time scale. Sindhwani et al. (2011) discussed the architecture of a tool and proposed a new family of low-rank matrix approximation algorithm on TFIDF model for modelling topics in a given social media corpus. Tan et al. (2011) showed that information about social relationship can be used to improve user-level sentiment analysis.

2.2 Citizen Social Sentiment Analysis for Government

As established in the facts presented in last section, social media presents itself as a '*big data*' source of citizen voice. If Government agencies can constantly keep a tab on pulse of its citizens, it can pave the way for better governance. Social sentiment analysis can be a very useful tool to achieve the same. It can address the following questions which Government agencies would be very interested to get an answer:

- How do **citizens feel** about the agency's new programmes and policies?
- What are the **most talked about programmes**? Is it **good or bad**?
- What are the **most positively** talked about attributes in the agency's programmes? Can the agency replicate it to other programmes?
- Is there **negative chatter** that the agency should respond to?
- Who are **advocates and sceptics** of the agency?
- Where the agency should be **actively listening**?

Answers to such questions would help agencies to fine-tune their policies to address specific concerns; transform their communication and out-reach programmes to clear any misconceptions; provide with insights on how its programmes and initiatives are perceived by its key stakeholders; identify best practices from positively perceived programmes and replicate it in others; design an effective performance model; and formulate a comprehensive social business strategy.

Interestingly, while it was well established for more than a decade that commercial organizations can get benefited from sentiment analysis (Zabin and Jefferies, 2008), its value for Governments was not very apparent until recent time.

In 2010, Gartner came up with Open Government Maturity Model (Maio, 2010). At 4th level of maturity, Gartner proposed sentiment analysis as a mean to achieve collaboration for Governments.

Echoing to that model, Forrester Research (Gliedman, 2011) observed that the US Federal government was monitoring the citizen sentiment in Twitter. Gartner (Maio, 2011) advised the Governments to use social media for achieving collaborative budgeting and pattern discovery where citizen sentiment analysis in social media can play a significant role. The public safety related works (Abbasi, 2007; and Bermingham et al., 2009) we mentioned in section 2.1, can be seen as early sentiment analysis related works for Government.

3 Approach

We could not find many publications that reported applying the social sentiment analysis in a Government context. Thus, it might be an opportune moment to attempt doing a sentiment analysis in the backdrop of a real-life Government problem. In this section, we proposed an approach to accomplish the same.

3.1 Topic Modelling Problem

Unlike few other type of content, such as movie review, social media is much unstructured and free flowing. Thus it is always a challenge to find out documents or entries that are relevant for the topic we are interested in. This relevance filtering based on topic can be seen as an Information

Extraction (IE) problem, where a large number of documents or entries in social media are analysed to extract some coherent topics out of it before further analysis for subjectivity detection and sentiment classification. This problem is called *Topic Modelling*.

The traditional Term Frequency and Inverted Document Frequency (TF-IDF) model, which is used in Information Retrieval (IR) for calculating relevance, can be adopted here though with some modification as explained below:

Let $X \in \mathbb{R}^{n \times m}$ be the document-term matrix that can be directly used in IR domain, where n = number of documents and m = number of terms. The elements of X can be defined as

$$X_{d,w} = \frac{\log(1 + tf_{d,w}) * idf_w}{C_d}$$

where $tf_{d,w}$ is the term frequency of term w in document d, $idf_w = \log(n / df_w)$, df_w is the document frequency of term w, and C_d is the normalizing factor. Dimensions of X are expected to be large in social media context though X is expected to be very sparsely populated.

If we want to learn k topics, then let $H \in \mathbb{R}^{k \times m}$ be the matrix of topics and terms. Similarly, we can imagine $W \in \mathbb{R}^{n \times k}$ as the matrix of topic distribution among documents. Thus the topic modelling problem can be reduced to be the problem of estimating W and H such that $WH \approx X$.

3.2 Architecture

In our approach, the topic modelling and sentiment analysis is performed by an IBM system – Cognos Consumer Insight (CCI). The architecture of CCI, which runs based on the theoretical foundation above, is presented at Figure 1. The components of this system are described below:

GPFS: The IBM General Parallel File System is a specialized file system targeted for high-performance applications – such as big data analytics.

Hadoop: Apache Hadoop is an open-source software framework for running data-intensive applications in a distributed fashion over commodity hardware.

SystemT: It is a rule-based IE system as proposed by Chiticariu et al. (2010). It uses a declarative rule language, AQL, to define the Natural Language Processing (NLP) rules for information extraction from documents.

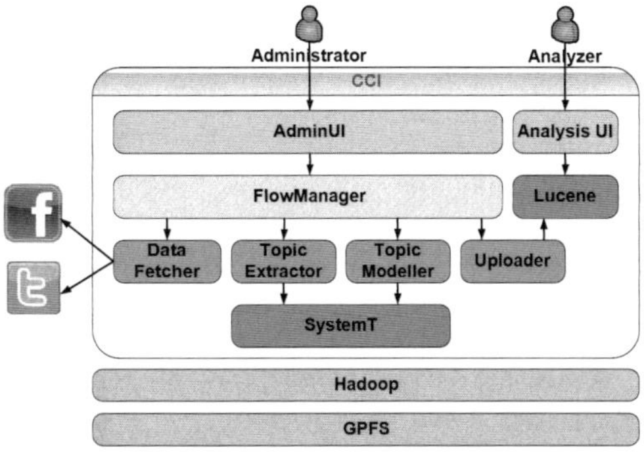

Figure 1: Cognos Customer Insight Architecture

FlowManager: Based on the rules and configurations, this component orchestrates the execution of different tasks across different components in this system.

Lucene: Apache Lucene is an open-source framework for IR applications.

AdminUI: The user interface used by administrators to configure this system and define AWL rules using simple interfaces.

AnalysisUI: The user interface component that enables sentiment analysis execution and rendering using Lucene component.

DataFetcher: The social media interfacing component that interacts with diverse sources, fetches information in different formats and produces JSON representation of them and saves into GPFS.

TopicExtractor: With the help of natural language processing rules in SystemT, this component extracts information from JSON data created by DataFetcher. It computes the $tf_{d,w}$ and idf_w values and produces X matrix. This component runs as a Hadoop job.

TopicModeller: This component computes the estimated matrices W and H. It employs the Proximal Rank-One Residue Iterations (Proximal-RRI) optimization algorithm as proposed by Sindhwani et al. (2011). It also produces JSON documents annotated with topic information. This component also runs as a Hadoop job.

Uploader: This component picks up the annotated JSON documents produced by TopicModeller and uploads them into a staging area. Lucene indexes these documents so that they can be searched and analysed based on extracted information using traditional sentiment analysis techniques for subjectivity detection and sentiment classification.

3.3 Method

We propose the three step method below:

Step I: Define Analysis Model. As first step the analysis model needs to be defined and configured through the AdminUI of CCI. The analysis model comprises of the following:

- **Query**: This defines the scope of baseline data retrieval from social media sources. The DataFetcher would use it. The result of the query produces the document dimension (n) of the W matrix.
- **Topic**: As explained earlier, it is important to define topics to bring the free-form large number of documents into a coherent group. The topics can be configured in CCI in two levels. A set of *Concept* terms are defined and those can be grouped into *Type*. These topics would be used by the analysis engine to create snippets of interest from the base list of documents retrieved from social media. For example, if we are analyzing a social services agency, all the benefit programmes such as Income Support, Employment Support can be identified as Concepts and grouped under the Topic 'Benefits'. This configuration would define the topic dimensions of W and H matrices.
- **Hotword**: Hotwords are the parameters that are common across the defined topics of interest. They can provide additional insight into how sentiments around a particular concept can be perceived in the context of different hotwords. For example, hotword can be a significant process step or a property that is common across multiple Government programmes. Some of the hotwords for a Social Services agency can be '*Claims*', '*Awareness*' etc. '*Income Support*' concept can be perceived in a negative sentiment in the context of *Claims* hotword, but can be perceived in a positive sentiment in the context of *Awareness* hotword.
- **Sentiment Lexicon**: Though CCI provides a sentiment lexicon assigned with prior polarity for different languages, it is necessary to validate that in the context of the rest of the analysis model. This is important since the connotation of a sentiment term can change depending on the context of analysis. Customisation can be done as necessary.

Step II: Perform Analysis. After configuration of the analysis model, the tool can be run and analysis can be performed across different dimensions. Some of them are presented in our *Result* section.

Step III: Root Cause Analysis. Once insights from the analysis are gained, a root cause analysis can be carried out. While this can be done manually by going through all the positive and negative sentiments and analyzing them, there are two ways we can get narrow down the root causes automatically with reasonable accuracy.

- By analyzing the hotwords and their associated overall sentiment that has a closer affinity with a concept. If a particular aspect has an overall negative sentiment and it has a closer affinity with a programme, then one of the root causes for that particular programme to have a negative sentiment is inefficiencies at that particular aspect of that programme.
- By extracting the *Title* of all the documents that contain a particular sentiment separately and by doing a *tag cloud* on the same, we can have some perspective on what discussion item is leading to most of the negative sentiment or a positive sentiment.

3.4 Experiment Setup

We performed Social Sentiment Analysis for one of the major social benefits organizations in the US. The scope included: (a) analysing agency's current social media presence and strategy and compare it with similar agencies in the world; (b) sentiment analysis to understand how agency's various benefit and healthcare programs are perceived by citizens; (c) identify root causes leading to the perceptions; and (d) preparing an actionable roadmap based on the findings.

We defined the boundary of our analysis as the user generated content between 1 Jun 2012 and 18 Oct 2012 from Twitter, Facebook, Flickr, YouTube, several blogs, forums and some general websites built around certain community. BoardReader crawler retrieved 41,405 documents based on our configured query and the analysis model extracted 16,954 snippets based on the topics defined. CCI version 1.1 was used to run the analysis.

4 Result

Results from Sentiment Analysis findings are presented below across various dimensions. Our interpretations of the results are also highlighted in the sections below.

4.1 Sentiment Distribution Across Concepts

This analysis is used to compare the perceived sentiments across concepts by citizens. This can be done at two levels:

- including sentiments from snippets that may or may not have hotwords; and
- including sentiments from snippets that has at least one occurrence of a hotword.

The 2nd level gives a much more focused perspective of sentiment analysis since it is relevant to the hotwords of interest.

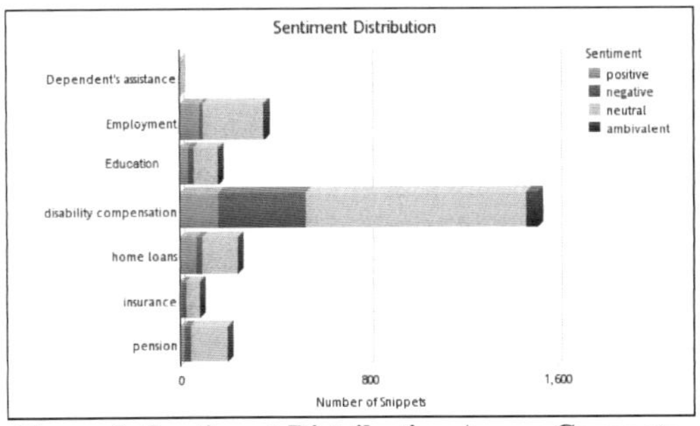

Figure 2: Sentiment Distribution Across Concepts (Regardless of Hotword Presence)

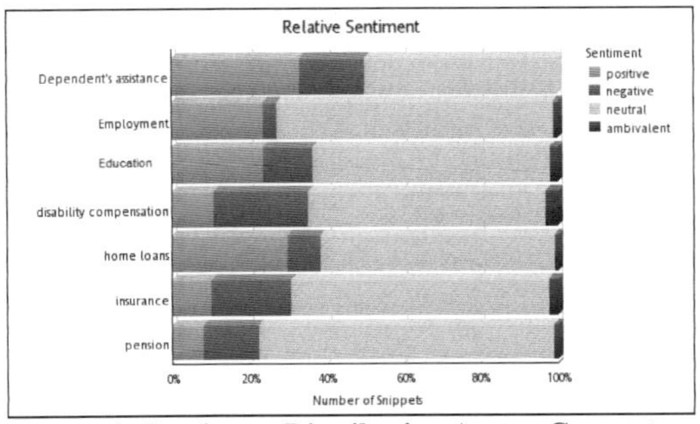

Figure 3: Sentiment Distribution Across Concepts (With Hotword Presence)

It is clearly evident that *Disability Compensation*, *Insurance*, and *Pension* contribute heavily towards negative sentiments, whereas *Employment Benefits*, *Dependent's Assistance*, and *Home Loan Benefits* are talked in positive light.

4.2 Sentiment Distribution Across Hotwords

This analysis gives a perspective on how various aspects of agency's programmes are perceived. The analysis is presented in Figure 4 and Figure 5. We observed the following: (a) *Claims* and *Awareness* are mostly associated with *Benefits and Services* programmes whereas *Quality* and *Helpline* are mostly associated with Healthcare programmes; and (b) *Claims* received most of the negative sentiments.

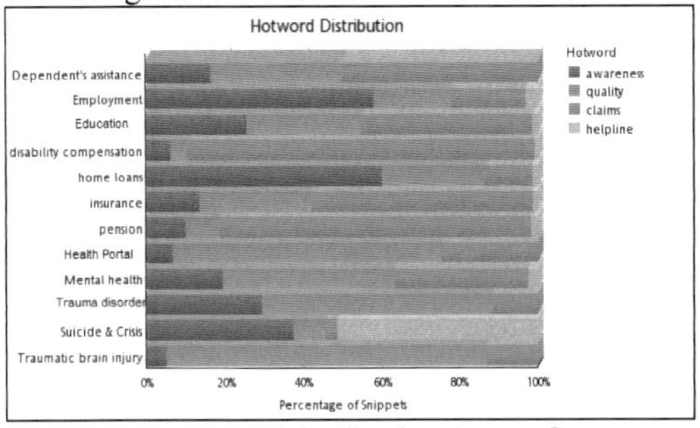

Figure 4: Hotword Distribution Across Concepts

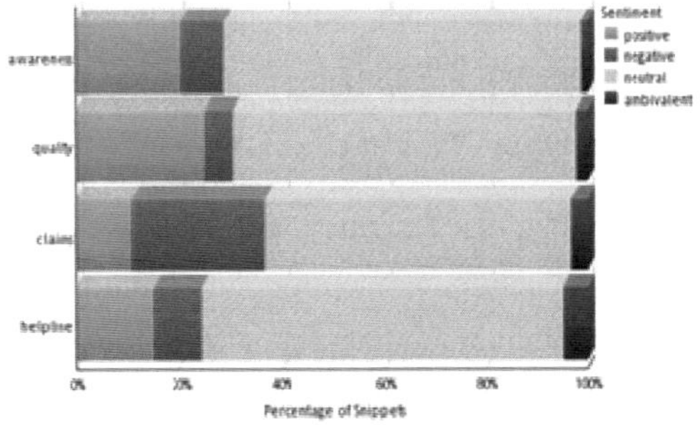

Figure 5: Sentiment Distribution Across Hotwords

4.3 Concept-Hotword Affinity Analysis

The relationship between Concepts and Hotwords is analyzed by measuring the degree of affinity between these two dimensions. It helps us derive which aspects of a particular programme lead to a particular sentiment thus giving some hints towards root cause. Chi-square distribution was used to measure the degree of affinity.

We observed the following: (a) *Disability Compensation* and *Pension* had a close affinity with *Claims*, which in turn had a negative sentiment due to high number of backlogs; (b) *Suicide and Crisis Prevention* had a high affinity with *Helpline* which had a positive sentiment; (c) *Mental Health* and other healthcare programmes had high affinity with *Quality* and were positively perceived; and (d) Many benefit programmes had close affinity with *Awareness*. There seemed to lot of out-reach activities done by the agency which boosted the positive sentiment around *Awareness*.

4.4 Root Cause Analysis

We performed a root cause analysis with the aid of affinity analysis and formation of tag cloud as shown below:

Figure 6: Tag Cloud

We discovered some of the major reasons behind negative sentiments: (a) the agency was suffering from huge backlogs in claims processing; (b) awareness of benefits and services was little among its clients and the agency needed to transform its outreach activities; and (c) agency had a poor social media strategy. This analysis provides key information to draw an actionable roadmap for the agency which can result in reducing negative perceptions and accentuating the positives.

5 Conclusion

In this work we chose a particular tool and proposed a method to apply social sentiment analysis in the context of Government. We went ahead and applied the technique and method to a real-life problem. In the process of doing so we gained valuable insights, which can be converted into actionable roadmap for the Government.

The success of this application can be taken as an encouragement to apply this approach to more such issues, such as – *Lokpal Bill* discussion in India or *Universal Credit* controversy in UK. Such analysis would be able to provide a conclusive sentimental insight from the mind of the citizens.

Another interesting problem that can be taken up is to apply this method in a multi-lingual country like India, where generating content in a mixture of languages (e.g. English and Bengali) is a common practice in social media.

References

A. Abbasi. 2007. *Affect intensity analysis of dark web forums.* Proceedings of Intelligence and Security Informatics (ISI), pp. 282–288

Sitaram Asur, and Bernardo A. Huberman. 2010. *Predicting the Future With Social Media.* Web Intelligence and Intelligent Agent Technology (WI-IAT), 2010 IEEE/WIC/ACM International Conference on. Vol. 1. IEEE

Adam Bermingham, Maura Conway, Lisa McInerney, Neil O'Hare, and Alan F. Smeaton. 2009. *Combining Social Network Analysis and Sentiment Analysis to Explore the Potential for Online Radicalisation.* International Conference on Advances in Social Network Analysis and Mining (ASONAM'09), IEEE

Johan Bollen, Alberto Pepe, and Huina Mao. 2011. *Modeling public mood and emotion: Twitter sentiment and socioeconomic phenomena.* Proceedings of the Fifth International AAAI Conference on Weblogs and Social Media.

Laura Chiticariu, Rajasekar Krishnamurthy, Yunyao Li, Sriram Raghavan, Frederick R. Reiss, and Shivakumar Vaithyanathan. 2010. *SystemT: an Algebraic Approach to Declarative Information Extraction.* Proceedings of the 48th Annual Meeting of the Association for Computational Linguistics, pp.128-137

Anthony R. Curtis. 2013. *The Brief History of Social Media.* University of North Carolina at Pembroke, [Online] Accessed on 1 Jun 2013 at http://www.uncp.edu/home/acurtis/NewMedia/SocialMedia/SocialMediaHistory.html

Chip Gliedman. 2011. *Industry Innovation: US Federal Government.* Forrester Research Report

Andrea Di Maio. 2010. *Gartner Open Government Maturity Model.* Gartner Report

Justin Martineau, and Tim Finin. 2009. *Delta tfidf: An improved feature space for sentiment analysis.* Proceedings of the 3rd AAAI International Conference on Weblogs and Social Media. 2009.

Alexander Pak, and Patrick Paroubek. 2010. *Twitter as a Corpus for Sentiment Analysis and Opinion Mining.* Proceedings of LREC. Vol. 2010

V. Sindhwani, A. Ghoting, E. Ting, and R. Lawrence. 2011. *Extracting insights from social media with large-scale matrix approximations.* IBM Journal of Research and Development, 55(5), pp.9:1-9:13

Chenhao Tan, Lillian Lee, Jie Tang, Long Jiang, Ming Zhou, and Ping Li. 2011. *User-level sentiment analysis incorporating social networks.* arXiv preprint arXiv:1109.6018

J. Zabin, and A. Jefferies. 2008. *Social media monitoring and analysis: Generating consumer insights from online conversation.* Aberdeen Group Benchmark Report

Modeling the Helpful Opinion Mining of Online Consumer Reviews as a Classification Problem

Yi-Ching Zeng
Department of Computer Science and Information Engineering
Chaoyang University of Technology, Taichung, Taiwan, R.O.C
st9506522@gmail.com

Shih-Hung Wu*
Department of Computer Science and Information Engineering
Chaoyang University of Technology, Taichung, Taiwan, R.O.C
shwu@cyut.edu.tw
*contact author

Abstract

The paper aims to address an opinion mining problem: to find the helpful reviews from online consumer reviews before mining the detail. This task can benefit both the consumers and the companies. Consumers can read only the helpful opinions from helpful reviews before they purchase a product, while the companies can acquire the true reason why one product is liked or hated. A system is built to assess the difficulty of the problem. The experiment results show that helpful reviews can be identified with high precision from unhelpful ones.

1 Introduction

Online consumer (or customer) review is a very important information source for many potential consumers to decide whether to buy or not. Li et al. (2011) shows that comparing to an expert product review "the consumer product review in the online shopping environment will be perceived by consumers to be more credible". This fact makes opinion mining on consumer reviews more interesting since it shows that opinions from other consumers are more helpful than those from experts. However, some reviews are not that helpful, as we can see from the vote of all readers on each consumer review on Amazon.com.

The paper aims to address an opinion mining problem: to find the helpful reviews from online consumers' reviews before mining the information from it. This task can benefit both the consumers and the companies. Consumers can read only the useful opinions from useful reviews before they purchase a product, while the companies can acquire the true reason why one product is liked or hated. Both save time from reading meaningless opinions that do not show good reasons. Figure 1 shows a clip image of an Amazon.com customer review. Each review has labeled the stars by the author and the number of people found the review helpful and the number of total number. A three-class classification problem is defined to model this application. A system is design to find the helpful positive reviews, for finding good reasons to buy a product; the helpful negative reviews, for finding reasons not to buy a product; and filtering out the unhelpful reviews no matter they are positive or negative.

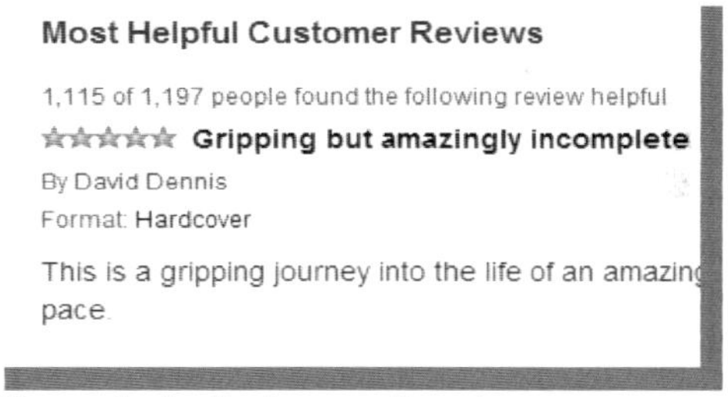

Figure 1: A clip image of an Amazon.com customer review.

The paper is organized as follows: Section 2 describes the features that can be used to classify the reviews into the helpful or the unhelpful ones. Section 3 describes the data collection of this study. Section 4 reports and discusses the experiment. The final section gives conclusions and future works.

IJCNLP 2013 Workshop on Natural Language Processing for Social Media (SocialNLP), pages 29–35,
Nagoya, Japan, 14 October 2013.

1.1 Related Works

Early works on opinion mining focused on the polarity of opinion, positive or negative, this kind of opinion mining was also called sentiment analysis. Another kind of opinion mining focused on finding the detail information of a product from reviews; such approach was a kind of information extraction (Hu & Liu, 2004). Recent researches focus on assessing the review quality before mining the opinion.

Kim et al. (2006) explored the use of some semantic features for review helpfulness ranking. They found that some important features of review, including *Length*, *Unigrams*, and *Stars* might provide the basis for assessing helpfulness of reviews.

Siersdorfer et al. (2010) presented a system that could automatically structure and filter comments for YouTube videos by analyzing dependencies between comments, views, comment ratings and topic categories. The method used the SentiWordNet thesaurus, a lexical WordNet-based resource containing semantic annotations. Moghaddam et al. (2011) proposed Matrix Factorization Model and Tensor Factorization Model for the prediction of the quality of online reviews, and evaluated the models by using a real life database from Epinions.com.

Lu (2010) exploited contextual information about authors' identities and social networks for improving review quality prediction. The method provided a generic framework for incorporating social context information by adding regularization constraints to the text-based predictor.

Xiong and Litman (2011) investigated the utility of incorporating additionally specialized features tailored to peer-review helpfulness. They found that structural features, review unigrams and meta-data combination were useful in modeling the helpfulness of both peer reviews and product reviews.

2 Classification Features

2.1 Manual Observation

Manual observation is necessary to find features for the helpful/unhelpful classification. Connors et al. (2011) gave a list on common ideas related to helpfulness and unhelpfulness, as shown in Table 1, which was collected from 40 students, each student reading 20 online reviews about a single product and giving comments on the reviews. The study provided 15 reasons that people think a consumer review helpful and 10 reasons of the unhelpful. These ideas can be viewed as features for a NLP classifier. However, some of them are hard to implement and require clear definition.

Helpfulness	**Times Mentioned**
Pros and Cons	36
Product Usage Information	30
Detail	24
Good Writing Style	13
Background Knowledge of Product	12
Personal Information About Reviewer	12
Comparisons	10
Lay-Man's Terms	9
Conciseness	8
Lengthy	7
Use of Ratings	7
Authenticity	5
Honesty	5
Miscellaneous	4
Unbiased	4
Accuracy	3
Relevancy	3
Thoroughness	3
Unhelpfulness	**Times Mentioned**
Overly Emotional/Biased	24
Lack of Information	17
Irrelevant Comments	9
Not Enough Detail	6
Poor Writing Style	6
Using Technical Language	6
Low Credibility	5
Problems With Quantitative Rating	5
Too Much Detail	5

Table 1: The 15 reasons that people think a customer review helpful and the 10 reasons of the unhelpful (Connors et al., 2011)

2.2 Features

Table 2 lists the features that we implement in this study. Comparing to the features used in previous works of Kim et al. (2006), we add more features based on the observation of Connors et al. (2011), especially the degree of detail.

The first three features are common n-gram used between a review and the corresponding product description. We believe that they are effective, since a good review should contain more relevant information and use exact terminology.

The fourth feature is the length of a review. A very short review cannot give much information and a long review might give more useful information. The fifth feature is whether the review compared something or not. A good review should compare the product to other similar product. Our program detects the string "compare to" or the pattern "ADJ+er than" exist in the review or not with the help of a list of comparative adjectives. The sixth feature is the degree of detail, which is a combination form of both length and n-gram. The degree of detail is not well-defined in previous work. Our definition is only a tentative one. We define the degree of detail of a review as:

$$log_{10}(\text{Product informatio n} + \text{Lengthy}) \quad (1)$$

where product information is the number of common words between a review and the corresponding product description. The seventh feature is the number of stars given by the review author. The eighth feature is whether the review contains "Pros" and "Cons" or not. Our system detects the string "Pros" and "Cons" existing in the review or not.

Feature	Description
Unigram(Product Description)	The number of unigram used between the review and the corresponding product description
Bigram (Product Description)	The number of Bigram used between the review and the corresponding product description
Trigram (Product Description)	The number of Trigram used between the review and the corresponding product description
Length	The length of a review
Comparisons	The review uses the string "compare to" or "ADJ + er than"
Degree of detail	Defined by formula (1)
Use of Ratings	The "Star" ratings of the review
Pros and Cons	The review contains exact the strings "Pros" and "Cons"

Table 2: 8 Features used in our system

3 Data Collection

In order to test the idea, we collect online customer reviews manually from Amazon.com in March and April 2013. The reviews are in eight different product domains: Book, Digital Camera, Computer, Foods & Drink, Movie, Shoes, Toys, and Cell-phone. We collect the first available 1000+ reviews with equal number of one to five stars without any special selection criterion in each domain. The average length is 80.63 words. The summery of our data collection is listed in Table 3.

The helpfulness score is given by the readers. As shown in Figure 1, the reviewer labeled the number of stars and other users voted the review as helpful or unhelpful. We take the confidence of being helpful as an index to sort the reviews. Figure 2 shows the distribution of polarity (form 1 to 5 star) and helpful/unhelpful confidence, where the y-axis is the confidence score. Note that the confidence score in previous work is defined as:

$$\text{Confidence} = 100\% \times \left(\frac{\text{Think helpful people}}{\text{Total people}} \right) \quad (2)$$

However, since there are some high confidence reviews with only very little support, the reviews might not be very helpful. We discount the confidence of them by redefining the confidence score as the log-support confidence (LSC):

$$\text{LSC} = log_{10}[(\#\text{of Think helpful people}) \times \left(\frac{\#\text{of Think helpful people}}{\#\text{of Total people}} \right)] \quad (3)$$

Figure 2 shows the data distribution. We can see that most reviews are positive and regard the helpfulness with high confidence. This fact shows that readers think other consumers are credible. The confidence of helpfulness is lower for the negative reviews. The confidence scores of each product domain are in Table 4.

3.1 Three-class classification problem

Instead of finding the correlation between the ranking of helpfulness and the prediction, we define the problem as a three class classification problem. The three-classes are: helpful positive reviews, for finding good reasons to buy a product; the helpful negative reviews, for finding reasons not to buy a product; and the unhelpful reviews.

Since there is no strong boundary between the helpful and the unhelpful, one purpose of the system is to filter out the most unhelpful reviews. The sizes of the three classes are adjusted by setting different thresholds. A higher threshold means to filter out more data. We can control the filtering level by setting different thresholds.

In our experiments, class 1 includes positive reviews with 4 or 5 stars and the helpfulness confidence is higher than threshold. Class 2 includes negative reviews with 1 to 3 stars and the helpfulness confidence is higher than the threshold. Class 3 is all the other reviews which are regarded as the unhelpful. The reviews that show no tendency to positive or negative are considered as the unhelpful.

Product	Reviews	Total Reviews Words	Average Length	s.d.
Book	1,065	93,497	87.79	1.8
Digital Camera	1,028	93,404	90.85	2.7
Computer	1,067	83,708	78.45	2.1
Foods & Drink	1,025	71,027	69.29	1.7
Movies	1,097	94,037	88.13	2.5
Shoes	1,000	75,237	75.23	1.6
Toys	1,100	85,196	77.45	1.7
Cell-Phone	1,308	101,957	77.88	2.0
Total / Average	8,690	884,964	80.63	2.02

Table 3: The summary of our data collection have 8 Classification and 8,690 reviews.

Product	Average LSC Confidence score
Book	1.134147
Digital Camera	1.37307
Computer	1.140333
Foods & Drink	0.931979
Movies	1.115796
Shoes	0.80848
Toys	0.806543
Cell-Phone	1.004922
Total average	1.03940875

Table 4: Eight Products for defined the LSC threshold in first experiment.

4 Experiment

The goal of the experiment is to test the difficulty of the three-class classification problem with different thresholds. We use the libSVM[1] toolkit to build the classifier based on the features described in section 2.2.

[1] http://www.csie.ntu.edu.tw/~cjlin/lib

4.1 Experiment design

We separate the data into training set and test set, each has 7,690 reviews and 1,000 reviews, respectively. The different thresholds tested in our experiment are: 1.039, 1.5, and 2.0. The first threshold is the average confidence score in Table 5, which filters out 56.1% of the reviews as the unhelpful; the second threshold 1.5, filters out 79.6%; and the third threshold 2.0, filters out 91.0%. The number of useful (both positive and negative) reviews of each product domain to the three threshold are listed in Table 5, 7, and 9. The sizes of classes corresponding to the three thresholds are show in Table 6, 8, and 10.

Product	Reviews
Book	522
Digital Camera	698
Computer	532
Foods & Drink	404
Movies	521
Shoes	246
Toys	318
Cell-Phone	571
Total Reviews	3,812

Table 5: Number of reviews over the threshold "1.039"

Classes	Reviews	%
Class 1 : Useful Positive	2,712	31.2%
Class 2 : Useful Negative	1,100	12.7%
Class 3 : Un-Useful	4,878	56.1%
Total Reviews	8,690	

Table 6: The size of the three classes with the threshold "1.039"

Product	Reviews
Book	270
Digital Camera	354
Computer	254
Foods & Drink	189
Movies	341
Shoes	49
Toys	174
Cell-Phone	139
Total Reviews	1,770

Table 7: Number of reviews over the threshold "1.5"

Classes	Reviews	%
Class 1 : Useful Positive	1,265	14.5%
Class 2 : Useful Negative	505	5.8%
Class 3 : Un-Useful	6,920	79.6%
Total Reviews	8,690	

Table 8: The size of the three classes with the threshold "1.5"

Product	Reviews
Book	129
Digital Camera	202
Computer	104
Foods & Drink	72
Movies	160
Shoes	9
Toys	73
Cell-Phone	32
Total Reviews	781

Table 9: Number of reviews over the threshold "2.0"

Classes	Reviews	%
Class 1 : Useful Positive	604	6.9%
Class 2 : Useful Negative	177	2.0%
Class 3 : Un-Useful	7,910	91.0%
Total Reviews	8,690	

Table 10: The size of the three classes with the threshold "2.0"

We conduct two experiments; the first one is a 10-fold validation on the training set, and the second one is a test on a separated test set.

4.2 Experiment Results

The average accuracy of the 10-fold cross validation result of each configuration is shown in Table 11. The 7,690 training data is separated into ten folds, and the system uses 90% of the data as the training set and the other 10% as the test set. A SVM classifier is trained in each fold and repeat 10 times. The result shows that with a higher threshold, 1.5 or 2.0, the accuracy of our system is about 72%.

Data set	Average Accuracy
LSC threshold 1.039	60.83%
LSC threshold 1.5	72.72%
LSC threshold 2.0	**72.82%**

Table 11: The average accuracy result of each data set in the ten-fold cross validation

In the second experiment, we use the 7,690 reviews as training set and test the classification on the 1,000 test set, where the number of test of each class is balanced to 1/3. Note that, the actual class of the test is fixed during the test, which is corresponding to a threshold 1.039. The classifier is trained with three different class distributions. The confusion matrix of our system is shown in Table 12 to 14. The precision and the recall of each class are also shown.

	Actual				
Predicted	Class 1	Class 2	Class 3	**Total**	**Precision**
Class 1	172	75	46	293	59%
Class 2	80	196	24	300	65%
Class 3	81	62	264	407	65%
Total	333	333	334	1,000	
Recall	52%	59%	79%		

Table 12: The confusion matrix (LSC threshold is over 1.039)

	Actual				
Predicted	Class 1	Class 2	Class 3	**Total**	**Precision**
Class 1	213	47	28	288	74%
Class 2	42	257	14	313	82%
Class 3	78	29	292	399	73%
Total	333	333	334	1,000	
Recall	64%	77%	87%		

Table 13: The confusion matrix (LSC threshold is over 1.5)

	Actual				
Predicted	Class 1	Class 2	Class 3	**Total**	**Precision**
Class 1	203	45	27	275	74%
Class 2	46	263	10	319	82%
Class 3	84	25	297	406	73%
Total	333	333	334	1,000	
Recall	61%	79%	89%		

Table 14: The confusion matrix (LSC threshold is over 2.0)

4.3 Discussion on the experiment result

Table 11 shows that the average accuracy numbers of the three data sets are 60.83%, 72.72%, and 72.82%. We find that when we set the threshold to 1.5 that is expected to prune 79.6%

of data; our system can get 72.72% accuracy on the helpful/unhelpful classification. This is a great reduce on human labor to find better mining candidates. We believe that, with proper number of training data, the accuracy should be around 75%. The accuracy can be higher with more features.

From the confusion matrix in Table 13, we find that, by choosing the threshold 1.5, our system can classify the three classes with precision 74%, 82%, and 73%; while the system recall for the three classes are 64%, 77%, and 87%. We can also find a similar result in Table 14, where the threshold is 2.0. The precision is almost the same, and the recall is different slightly.

5 Conclusion and Future Works

The paper reports how a system can find helpful online reviews and is tested on the three-class classification problem. The threshold of the helpful/unhelpful can be decided according to the amount of data that the users want to prune. The overall accuracy of three-class problem is about 73%. Helpful negative reviews can be found with 82% precision and 77% recall. Helpful positive reviews can be found with 74% precision and 64% recall. Unhelpful reviews can be filtered out automatically from all the consumer reviews with a high recall rate about 87% and 73% precision. Considering the original distribution (20% as useful), the system performance is quite highCurrently, our system is based on features observed by human in previous works and we only implement some of them. In the future, we will try to implement more features and to extract features from the training corpus automatically.

Acknowledgement

This study was financially supported by the Research Grant NSC 102-2221-E-324 -034 from Taiwan's National Science Council.

References

Laura Connors, Susan M. Mudambi, and David Schuff. 2011. *Is it the Review or the Reviewer? A Multi-Method Approach to Determine the Antecedents of Online Review Helpfulness*, Proceedings of the 2011 Hawaii International Conference on Systems Sciences (HICSS), January.

Minqing Hu and Bing Liu. 2004. *Mining opinion features in customer reviews*. In Proceedings of the 19th national conference on Artifical intelligence (AAAI'04), Anthony G. Cohn (Ed.). AAAI Press 755-760.

Soo-Min Kim, Patrick Pantel, Tim Chklovski, Marco Pennacchiotti. 2006. *Automatically Assessing Review Helpfulness,* Proceedings of the 2006 Conference on Empirical Methods in Natural Language Processing, pp.423—430.

M. Li, L. Huang, C. Tan, and K. Wei. 2011. *Assessing The Helpfulness Of Online Product Review: A Progressive Experimental Approach,* In Proceedings of PACIS.

Yue Lu, Panayiotis Tsaparas, Alexandros Ntoulas, Livia Polanyi. 2010. *Exploiting Social Context for Review Quality Prediction*, Proceedings of the 19th international conference on World wide web pp. 691-700.

Samaneh Moghaddam, Mohsen Jamali, Martin Ester. 2010. *Review Recommendation: Personalized Prediction of the Quality of Online Reviews*, Proceedings of the 20th ACM international conference on Information and knowledge management pp.2249-2252.

Susan M. Mudambi, and David Schuff. 2010. *What Makes a Helpful Online Review? A Study of Customer Reviews on Amazon.com,* MIS Quarterly, (34: 1) pp.185-200.

Stefan Siersdorfer, Sergiu Chelaru, Jose San Pedro. 2010. *How useful are your comments?: analyzing and predicting youtube comments and comment ratings,* Proceedings of the 19th international conference on World wide web pp.891-900.

Wenting Xiong, Diane Litman. 2011. *Automatically Predicting Peer-Review Helpfulness*, Proceedings of the 49th Annual Meeting of the Association for Computational Linguistics: short papers, pp. 502–507.

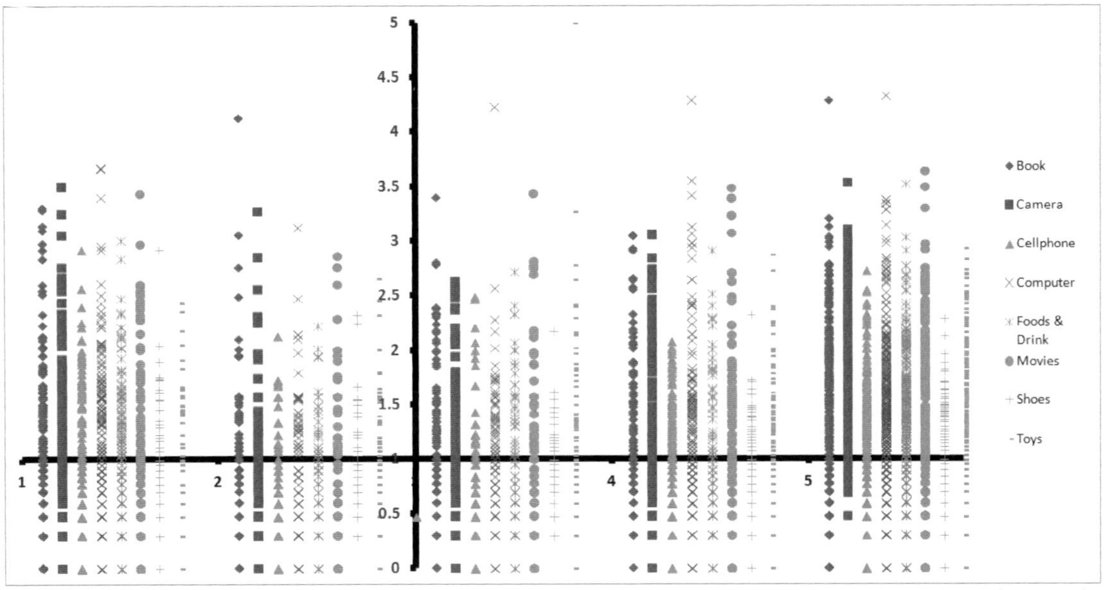

Figure 2: Stars vs. helpfulness distribution of our data collection. The x-axis is the number of stars of customer reviews; the y-axis is the confidence score LSC.

Trust Evaluation Mechanisms for Wikipedia

Imran Latif
PUCIT, University of the Punjab
Lahore, Pakistan
mscsf11m015@pucit.edu.pk

Syed Waqar Jaffry
PUCIT, University of the Punjab
Lahore, Pakistan
swjaffry@pucit.edu.pk

Abstract

Wikipedia is the well-nigh successful and most popular free encyclopedia developed by many editors in collaborative manner. It provides multitude of opportunities for online large scale knowledge sharing between virtual communities by letting the viewer to create and edit articles directly in the web browser. Information on Wikipedia is expanding largely, but the increase in quantity is not proportional to quality of the content. The cursory observer of Wikipedia may not be able to differentiate between the good and the bad quality of the content. Despite the success of Wikipedia, trust on Wikipedia content is still questioned because of its open editing model. In this paper primarily the challenges for trust evaluation mechanisms, caused by the significant characteristics of Wikipedia's knowledge base are discussed. Existing Wikipedia trust evaluation models are comprehensively surveyed and key issues related to these are highlighted. Finally based on this study new dimensions for effective trust evaluation mechanisms are proposed, which are aimed to setup clear goals for future research in this area.

1 Introduction

Recently an average web user has been emerged from a consumer to a content creator after the advent of Web 2.0. So a large volume of content is generated on web that is driven by the open collaborative model and mutual contributions on the social media like Wikis, Blogs and Social Networks. The gateways to access these contents are well known search engines. But they don't provide guarantee about the trustworthiness of knowledge present at Web. So it has become very important to evaluate the trustworthiness of the content that is produced by unknown users.

Wikipedia ranks as one of the top ten most visited web sites (Javanmardi, Ganjisaffar, Lopes, and Baldi, 2011) on Web which is a most successful and well known User Generated Content (UGC) repository. Various studies have been constituted to evaluate the trust in Open Collaborative Authoring System (OCAS) e.g. Wikipedia. Trust of readers on the information presented in these open content knowledge bases is often wondered and questioned (Moturu and Liu, 2009) by researchers. The quality of Wikipedia contents is not guaranteed as vandalism and manipulation cannot completely be eradicated. Hence several researchers have focused to minimize vandalism through fostering readers trust on content through the analysis of Wikipedia editor's behavior and the text's quality (Adler, Alfaro, and Pye, 2010). Wikipedia is designed in such a way that it has fresh information content rather than existing encyclopedias, because the editors at Wikipedia are more active and many in numbers. This largest encyclopedia is based on crowd sourcing (Fuchs, 2008). It is a system in which there is an open call of outsourcing to large group of people for completion on a specific task.

Primary goal of this paper is to provide a comprehensive summary and a comparison of the features used in identification of trust evaluation mechanisms, presented in literature for Wikipedia contents. These features are grounded and have foundations in the domain of open collaborative systems (Waltinger, Breuing, and Wachsmuth, 2011). Another significant contribution of this work is the categorization of the trust evaluation methods in field of Wikipedia and the provision of a comprehensive coverage of the open problems in this domain. This list of the open problems provides an agenda for researchers in this area.

Residuum of this paper is coordinated as follows. Section II introduces important terminology and concepts, as well summarize the problem of trust in contrast with various systems, it also introduce enduring examples in domain. Section III highlights several areas and follow-ups in more detail to the logical fundament of the trust evaluation for Wikipedia knowledge base. Section IV reviews several trust evaluation mechanisms and propose the open challenges in this field. Finally section V concludes this paper.

IJCNLP 2013 Workshop on Natural Language Processing for Social Media (SocialNLP), pages 36–42,
Nagoya, Japan, 14 October 2013.

2 Background

Wikipedia can be viewed as an electronic session for brain storming between the colleagues or likeminded individuals, but some others heavily criticized on the open editing natures of Wikipedia and found it as waste of time (Gorman, 2005). In (West, Weber, and Castillo, 2012) Wikipedians characteristics and their editing behavior in context of their online activities beyond the Wikipedia are studied. It is found that Wikipedia editors play more games, read more news, do more search and mostly indulge in pop culture. Wikipedia's article become good quality or feature article in a short time span, especially those in which editors take more participation (Nemoto, Gloor, and Laubacher, 2011). Talk pages at Wikipedia for article can be also be simulated to make the social network between editors and to do their mutual interaction. There are certain key findings about Wikipedians, the most important findings are that they start in intense manner, tail of little, and then they maintain relatively high activity in the rest of their career (Panciera, Halfaker, and Terveen, 2009).

Information risks associated with the Wikipedia articles determine that the articles may also contain information that is not reliable and readers can't trust on it. So there is a possibility that intentionally false information is added there (Denning, Horning, Parnas, and Weinstein, 2005). More precisely, risks associated with the Wikipedia articles are classified in (Denning, Horning, Parnas, and Weinstein, 2005). These risks are equally applicable on all the systems that are open and users generated contents.

To evaluate the reliability of the content of Wikipedia in this paper primary focus is on terms of "Trustworthiness" and "Trust". It is also well accepted that the most important concept during the transaction between two entities is the trust between trustor and trustee (B. Bailey, L. Gurak, and J. Konstan, n.d.). Trust is defined as a degree by which trustee is able to satisfy the anticipation about a risk involving in transaction for a trustor. In this paper focus is on the perspective of the trustor, which relies on the quantity of trust affiliated with the trustee.

2.1 Trust Management

Trust fostering in open content systems can only be done by an efficient Trust management for readers or users. Trust management is defined by (Grandison and Sloman, 2003) as follows,

> "The activity of collecting, codifying, analyzing and presenting evidence relating to competence, honesty, security or dependability with the purpose of making assessments and decisions regarding trust relationships for Internet applications".

The best practices for the trust management and to enhance the trust online is providing the feedback about the content (Shneiderman, 2000).

2.2 Parameters for Trust Evaluation

There are several factors that can be used to evaluate the trust of users on the content that is generated in a collaborative manner. The two most important parameters to evaluate the trust of users are quality and credibility of the content, explanation of these parameters is as follows:

1) Quality: One can define quality of the text as an essential character or inherent feature for trust. To evalauet the quality some predictors can also be used to to derived quality from the content. There are many other aspects in the definition of quality e.g. expertise, correctness and credibility. In literature one of the primary approche to measure the quality of the Wikipedia content is using survival and link ratio as presented in (Adler et al., 2008a). Sometime trust is also used interchangeably with quality but it is important to understand that these two issues are distinct (Lampe, Doupi, and Van den Hofen, 2003).

2) Credibility: Quality of the inspiring belief is define as Credibility (Moturu and Liu, 2009). The most suitable property about credible content is it's factual accuracy. In open editing models, metadata associated with the content is the best source to judge this attribute. In Wikipedia domain metadata information e.g. proportion of reverted edits, revision counts, edit length, mean time between successive edits and reverted edits can be used to measure this trust evalution parameter.

3 Trust Evaluation Mechanisms in Wikipedia

To evaluate the trust on the text and its authors and/or editors, one needs to assess the material authenticity and the reputation of the authors and/or editors. In this section the methods for the trust evaluation are categorized and limitations of these categories are described briefly. A summary of the methods is also presented in Table 1.

3.1 Quantitative Evaluation

Quantitative analysis of the Wikipedia data and analyzing the trust using existing data of the Wikipedia can be performed through tracing the author's activity from database dumps. In (Ortega and Barahona, 2007) is found that editing behavior of authors change over time. It is also stated that the analysis of sysops (an administrator of a multi-user computer system) is not much effective to analyze the contribution because the policy at Wikipedia to elect them is also continuously evolving in collaborative manner. Automated computation of the trust (Zeng, Alhossaini, Ding, Fikes, and McGuinness, 2006a) is proposed with the help of revision history of an article that is basically developed through the help of Dynamic Bayesian Network (DBN) and its outcome is a trust evaluation model that evaluates trust on a Wikipedia article.

Another trust evaluation model (Zeng, Alhossaini, Fikes, and McGuinness, 2006) is presented that is also based on article revision history. This model uses article fragments to evaluate trust. It also explores the dynamic nature of revisions so that revision history can be best utilized. This model calculates the trust on the fragments of an article. In comparison to the citation-based model (McGuinness et al., 2006) to evaluate the trust this model performs far better.

Basic limitations in above described models are that if there are no edits on articles in long time by editor then these models assume that the great degree of personal belief exists in that particular article which is not universal true. Trust labeling by the techniques described above are also unable to consider the change in positioning of words during edits. They measure each edit at granularity of sentence hence inherently these techniques miss the important aspect of positioning and in that consequence may lead to calculate distrust by these methods. Text deletions edges for cut-and-paste are also not labeled for trust evaluation which means that when the text is removed and added again in an article then it is calculated as a new edit that is another limitation of models described above.

3.2 Qualitative Evaluation

There are always a large number of collaborative activities involved in an open editing model when used over the internet. To answer the trust assessment doubts about collaboratively generated content, quality of the content becomes a prime question. Statistical analysis of the Wikipedia (Wilkinson and Huberman, 2007) has shown that presumably high-quality featured articles can be distinguished on the basis of the number of edits and contributions made by various authors/editors. In (Stvilia, Twidale, Gasser, and Smith, 2005) information quality is measured using process-oriented pages (e.g. discussion pages about the editing process). According to them it helps to understand the discussions at talk pages about edits, and other tradeoffs they make between these dimensions also enables one to assess the quality.

Evolution of content quality is modeled in (Javanmardi and Lopes, 2010) for the Wikipedia articles to evaluate the time fractions in which articles obtained and retained high quality condition. A trust evaluation system is designed in combination of link analysis method and text survival ratio (Suzuki and Yoshikawa, 2012). This system basically evaluates the quality of articles by mutually evaluating the parameters about text and editors. When text is able to survive within the multiple revisions of article then it is considered as good quality text by them.

Another trust model is proposed in (Moturu and Liu, 2009) that relies on author's information and revision history of content. Their method has three major steps for trust evaluation which are described as follow:

- Features are indentified that are capable to judge the trust of user on content.
- Trust evaluation models are designed that are feature-driven and independent of application as well.
- Evaluation of performance is done for such models.

Study on the impact of press citation is done in (Lih, 2004) for the computation of quality to a Wikipedia article in terms of number of edits and their particular impacts. They concluded that reputation of an article can be benchmarked by analysis of metadata without the rendering of article content.

One can also get the reputation of authors to evaluate the trust on individuals in the form of feedback (Adler et al., 2008a) of readers about authors, but this mechanism about individuals is missing here. External citation perspective is also missing in the above defined methods for measuring the quality of text. Because if text is cited outside the Wikipedia in some domain specific resource or at well known research repository, then it may means that particular article has good quality text. Moreover the sources verification process belonging to an article is also very significant to evaluate the trust on article as well to measure the quality of text that is also major lacking area of researches in qualitative evaluation.

3.3 Collaborative Information Repository's Perspective in Trust Evaluation

Wikipedia is based on open editing model which is developed in collaborative manner in which an article written and edited by several contributors. In such system reputation of authors is very important and their collaboration matters are also considerably important in trust evaluation of content (Zeng, Alhossaini, Fikes, and McGuinness, 2006).

In (McGuinness et al., 2006) revision history is used to evaluate the trust on author. It is found that the reputation of an author affects the trust on article. Their method is based on an assumption that one article is edited by multiple authors and here each edit is called a fragment. Trust is basically computed on the basis of citation and link ratio. Following steps are proposed by them to calculate the trust associated with a fragment from an article,

- Identify authors of the article and compute the trust for each author.
- Find the provenance information about edit. Here PML (Proof Markup Language) is proposed for this purpose.
- Calculate the trust on each author, independent of data storage without using Wikipedia components.

Citation of an article is considered in two ways by them; in first, if article is referred in another article then referred article gain positive trust. In second way non-citation occurrences are count. Finally page Rank algorithm is used to evaluate the trust that finds citation for particular article. They concluded that no single technique between the citation and page rank gives best results, so hybrid techniques that include PML in combination can be used for better results.

Another model of Trust evaluation is presented in (Adler et al., 2008a) that is based on revision history and reputation of authors that contributes in content generation process. In this model, trust on each word of article is calculated based on two things. One is the reputation of authors that writes particular word, and other is reputation of editors who edits nearby words. In (Adler and Alfaro, 2007) reputation of author is measured by their text age and survival ratio. This method is resistant to tampering as it has no affect of deleting and re-insertion of text by vandals. Authors that gain the high reputation, mostly generate the high quality content and this high quality content survive for long time; this intuition is also confirmed by (Adler, De Alfaro, Pye, and Raman, 2008b).

Major limitation of fragment based methods is that overall quality of the article becomes black box. Because trust of fragments and authors is calculated as fragment-of-article or author-to-fragment graphs. The link ratio base method has also limitation, that some newly written article may have more non-cited references. Another limitation of the proposed survival ratio based methods is that they work better on few articles which were highly modified by editors. This condition is not always meets when an article has low edits.

Limitations of Feedback based Trust Models: There are questions raised in mind that why not we use feedback model to calculate the degrees of quality related to text. Answer to this question is that, open edit system is itself kind of peer review system as editor's vote for implicit features of articles (Stvilia, Twidale, Smith, and Gasser, 2008). An implementation of voting systems is implemented based on MediaWiki (Wikipedia' English version for educational purposes) which is named as "Article Feedback Tool" (Kramer, Gregorowicz, and Iyer, 2008). The major limitation with these feedback models are that every users does not evaluate or review properly. In fact, according to a study (MG Siegler, n.d.) about YouTube statistics stated, voters mostly give highest votes to videos whenever they vote. So we can conclude that user usually rates for good targets.

3.4 User's Behaviours Perspective in Trust Evaluation

Content in Wikipedia is basically the result of collaborative contributions of several contributors, so the perspective of Wikipedia contributors (reader, patroller, author, editor, admin etc) is very important. Some of these contributors, self-proclaimed "patrollers" are continuously watching the article to maintain its integrity by correcting or removing the content from the article. To help these patrollers, multi-agent cognitive based trust model (Krupa, Vercouter, Hübner, and Herzig, 2009) is proposed. It assists patroller and reducing their load as well as provides them aid regarding decision making for trust evaluation on editors/author's effort. In order to maintain the social control a Multi-agent trust model approach can perform better as it enables the system for trust evaluation of other agents with in a system. One of such model is the ForTrust model that is also inspired by the theory of Social Trust presented in (B. Bailey, L. Gurak, and J. Konstan, n.d.).

In (Javanmardi, Ganjisaffar, Lopes, and Baldi, 11) analysis is performed for trust evaluation using statistical methods considering the perspectives of registered and anonymous contributors. Power law behavior is suggested by these results of submission by registered and anonymous contributors. It is observed that 7% of contributions submitted the revisions in which most of them are registered, for almost 80% of whole revisions. So, it could be summarized that 63.94% of contributions in revisions are submitted by registered contributors. An interesting factor is also revealed regarding registered contributor's perspective, that only 10% revisions are submitted by administrators and 5.5% are submitted by Bots. It is observed that feature articles are formed in result of continuous effort by experienced contributors that has high reputation (Stein and Hess, 2007), hence it does matter a lot who has contributed.

3.5 Trust Fostering Policies and Visualization Impact on Readers Trust

Trustworthiness tool's impact for Wikipedia is calculated in (Kittur, Suh, and Chi, 20008). They study the effectiveness of trust evaluation methods that how much these tools affect on reader's trust about the Wikipedia's article. It is also measured that either the visualization impacts the user's perception or not by showing them hidden information about the article e.g. text quality. It is found that visualization of editor's behavior, edit patterns and stability of article impacts on reader's trust.

Another model named WikiTrust is proposed (Zhao, Kallander, Gbedema, Johnson, and Wu, 2011b) that take advantage of social context. It includes the social relation and background information of editors and conveys it to readers with personalized and authentic information. In (Lucassen and Schraagen, 2011a) it is found that the best mechanism for trust evaluation is to use multiple methods as no single method provides all possible information for trust evaluation. Several methods are combined by them with Wikipedia Screening Task. They found that combination of these methods improve results. Three experimental approaches are proposed namely eye-tracking, online questionnaires and think aloud.

Trust of reader can also be fostered by enforcing the security policies so that readers believe that there is a proper procedure of content generation and verification. Such a security policy is propped in (Lindberg and Jensen, 2012) to enforce the integrity of content in comparison to existing Wikipedia security policy to enhance the trust of the user on information. Visualization model WikiTrust (Lucassen and Schraagen, 2011b) also helps reader in order to identify the trustworthiness of content by coloring the background of less trustworthy word with some specific colors.

Trust Evaluation Mechanisms Category	Trust Evaluation Mechanisms Techniques
Quantitative Perspective	Models based on revision history using Dynamic Bayesian Network
	Models based on revision history and article fragments
	Citation-based model
	Models based on statistical analysis of the Wikipedia
Qualitative Perspective	Models based on process-oriented pages e.g. discussion pages
	Model based on content quality (used in CalSWIM mashup as a case study)
	Model based on link analysis method and text survival ratio
	Techinque based on dispersion degree score (DDS) and Normalized Discounted Cumulative Gain (NDCG)
	Model based on number of edits and their impacts
Collaborative Information Repository's Perspective	Model based on editors/authors reputation and their collaboration matters
	Model based on combination of revision history, link ratio and PML (Proof Markup Language)
	Model based on revision history and reputation of authors
	Model based on text age and survival ratio
User's Behaviour Perspective	Techniques based on Multi-agent cognition based trust model (ForTrust model based techniques)
	Model based on perspectives of registered and anonymous contributors
Trust Fostering Policies and Visualization Perspective	Techniques based on visualizations impact on Trust
	Techniques based on social context including social relation
	Techniques based on security policy

Table 1. Trust Evaluation Mechanisms Summary

4 Open Problems in Trust Evaluation on Wikipedia

There are several problems in the domain of trust evaluation which are still to be investigated are described as follows:

1) Vagueness of Quality: Survival ratio of editing text is a significant factor to evaluate the quality of text in the trust evaluation process for articles (Suzuki and Yoshikawa, 2012). There is supposition in this technique that article may have long editing history for finding of editor's and text quality. This technique performs well when article has long editing history but when editors edits rarely because of any reason then there is chance that particular article's text obtain high quality which is not the actual case. Hence there is need to adress such problems.

2) Trust Evaluation using Natural Language Processing Techniques: In several research articles primary focus is on survival ratio by counting the words to evaluate the quality. So the importance of linguistic structure is missing there e.g. sentences "B is A" and "B is not A" have only one additional word added but meaning is totally changed, so the analysis of text using NLP means a lot. Moreover, it is also established (Sabel, 2007) that analysis of text is very important in finding the text qualities. This is the major lacking area in preovious researches which should be addressed.

3) User Interface and Visualization: Several researcher have focused to evaluate the trust on Wikipedia content but very less focus is given to find the impact of these models on reader's trust. It is observed that user's trust level about the content changes when trust is shown to user with help of good visualization.

4) Credibility of References: Currently if a Wikipedia article has external references then usually it is considered as a good quality article but it is not necessary that provided source is a valid and well related in the context. So in general the credibility of sources is lacking in the Wikipedia.

5) Structure of the Content: Structure of the content related to Wikipedia's article is also significant factor of that can provide a quality measurement. Current literature rarely focuses on this aspect. These aspects include that whether the data is well structured and organized or not, it has balanced material or not, or it contains the images and tables to support material facts and their demonstration.

6) Social Context: To evaluate the trust existing literature focused on the author's behavior mostly within the domain of Wikipedia while they lack the significant aspect of social context outside the domain of Wikipedia to evaluate the behavior of author/editor. A study (Suh, Chi, Kittur, and Pendleton, 2008) also states that distrust on mutable social collaborative systems such as Wikipedia can be reduced by providing readers with transparency about contributors and content generation process.

7) Sentiment Context: Sentiment context mean that what sentiment other user's have about a particular author during any transaction e.g. other authors may think that the author has positive/negative/neutral attitude towards a topic or an article. In social environment the attitude of individual towards each others can be used for predicting their negative and positive attitude as well (Sepehri Rad, Makazhanov, Rafiei, and Barbosa, 2012). Sentiment context is also lacking area that can also be evaluated with the help of material logged in talk pages to evaluate the sentiment of other authors about particular topic.

5 Discussions and Conclusion

Wikipedia is most viewed and largest encyclopedic knowledge reference and it is also in list of the top ten most visited web resources (Alexa., n.d.). Wikipedia has still more reliable information irrespective of its open editing model (Giles, 2005). It is found that Wikipedia has slightly more faults (approximately 4 to every 3) than the Encyclopedia Britannica for a particular sample distribution of scientific articles. So we can say that Wikipedia is still mostly referred source for information gain.

It this article a brief survey on trust evaluation strategies and mechanism in the domain of Wikipedia is provided. The opportunities and challenges in this area are described as well as the limitations of existing models are also analyzed and presented. A list of open problems in this area is also proposed so that researchers can determine particular goals future research.

References

Adler, B. T., and Alfaro, L. de. (2007). A content-driven reputation system for the Wikipedia. In Proceedings of the 16th international conference on World Wide Web (pp. 261–270). Banff, Alberta, Canada: ACM.

Adler, B. T., Chatterjee, K., Alfaro, L. de, Faella, M., Pye, I., and Raman, V. (2008a). Assigning trust to Wikipedia content. In Proceedings of the 4th International Symposium on Wikis (pp. 1–12). Porto, Portugal: ACM.

Adler, B. T., De Alfaro, L., Pye, I., and Raman, V. (2008b). Measuring author contributions to the Wikipedia. In Proceedings of the 4th International Symposium on Wikis (pp. 15:1–15:10). New York, NY, USA: ACM.

Adler, B. T., Alfaro, L. de, and Pye, I. (2010). Detecting Wikipedia Vandalism Using WikiTrust.

Alexa. (n.d.). The top 500 sites on the web. Retrieved from http://www.alexa.com/topsites

B. Bailey, L. Gurak, and J. Konstan. (n.d.). Trust in cyberspace. Human factors and Web development.

Denning, P., Horning, J., Parnas, D., and Weinstein, L. (2005). Wikipedia risks. Commun. ACM, 48(12), 152–152.

Fuchs, C. (2008). Don Tapscott y Anthony D. Williams. Wikinomics: How mass Collaboration changes Everything. International Journal of Communication, (2), 1–11.

Giles, J. (2005). Internet encyclopaedias go head to head. Nature, 438(7070), 900–901.

Gorman, G. E. (2005). Editorial: Is the wiki concept really so wonderful? Online Information Review, 29(3), 225–226.

Grandison, T., and Sloman, M. (2003). Trust management tools for internet applications. In Proceedings of the 1st international conference on Trust management (pp. 91–107). Heraklion, Crete, Greece: Springer-Verlag.

Javanmardi, S., and Lopes, C. (2010). Statistical measure of quality in Wikipedia. In Proceedings of the First Workshop on Social Media Analytics (pp. 132–138). New York, NY, USA: ACM. Javanmardi, S., Ganjisaffar, Y., Lopes, C., and Baldi, P. (11). User contribution and trust in Wikipedia (pp. 1–6). Presented at the Collaborative Computing: Networking, Applications and Worksharing, 2009. 5th International Conference on CollaborateCom 2009.

Kittur, A., Suh, B., and Chi, H. (2008). Can you ever trust a wiki?: impacting perceived trustworthiness in Wikipedia. In Proceedings of the 2008 ACM conference on Computer supported cooperative work (CSCW '08). ACM, New York, NY, USA, 477-480.

Kramer, M., Gregorowicz, A., and Iyer, B. (2008). Wiki trust metrics based on phrasal analysis. In Proceedings of the 4th International Symposium on Wikis (pp. 1–10). Porto, Portugal: ACM.

Krupa, Y., Vercouter, L., Hübner, J., and Herzig, A. (2009). Trust Based Evaluation of Wikipedia's Contributors. In H. Aldewereld, V. Dignum, and G. Picard (Eds.), Engineering Societies in the Agents World X (Vol. 5881, pp. 148–161). Springer Berlin Heidelberg.

Lampe, K., Doupi, P., and Van den Hofen, J. M. (2003). Internet health resources: from quality to trust. Methods of Information in medicine, 42(2), 134–142.

Lindberg, K., and Jensen, C. D. (2012). Collaborative trust evaluation for wiki security. In Proceedings of the 2012 Tenth Annual International Conference on Privacy, Security and Trust (PST) (pp. 176–184). Washington, DC, USA: IEEE Computer Society. Lih, A. (2004). Wikipedia as Participatory journalism: reliable sources? metrics for evaluating collaborative media as a news resource. Proceedings of Fifth International Symposium on Online Journalism, April 16-17, 2004, (Austin, TX).

Lucassen, T., and Schraagen, J. M. (2011a). Researching Trust in Wikipedia. In: Chi Sparks 2011, June 23, 2011, Arnhem, the Netherlands.

Lucassen, T., and Schraagen, J. M. (2011b). Evaluating WikiTrust: A Trust Support Tool for Wikipedia. First Monday, 16(5).

McGuinness, D. L., Zeng, H., Silva, P. P. da, Ding, L., Narayanan, D., and Bhaowal, M. (2006). Investigation into trust for collaborative information repositories: A Wikipedia case study. In Proceedings of the Workshop on Models of Trust for the Web.

Moturu, S. T., and Liu, H. (2009). Evaluating the trustworthiness of Wikipedia articles through quality and credibility. In Proceedings of the 5th International Symposium on Wikis and Open Collaboration (pp. 1–2). Orlando, Florida: ACM.

MG SIEGLER. (n.d.). YouTube Comes To A 5-Star Realization: Its Ratings Are Useless.

Nemoto, K., Gloor, P., and Laubacher, R. (2011). Social capital increases efficiency of collaboration among Wikipedia editors. In Proceedings of the 22nd ACM conference on Hypertext and hypermedia (pp. 231–240). Eindhoven, The Netherlands: ACM.

Ortega, F., and Barahona, J. M. G. (2007). Quantitative analysis of thewikipedia community of users. In Proceedings of the 2007 international symposium on Wikis (pp. 75–86). Montreal, Quebec, Canada: ACM.

Panciera, K., Halfaker, A., and Terveen, L. (2009). Wikipedians are born, not made: a study of power editors on Wikipedia. In Proceedings of the ACM 2009 international conference on Supporting group work (pp. 51–60). Sanibel Island, Florida, USA: ACM.

Sabel, M. (2007). Structuring wiki revision history (pp. 125–130). Presented at the WikiSym'07: Proceedings of the 2007 international symposium on Wikis, ACM.

Sepehri Rad, H., Makazhanov, A., Rafiei, D., and Barbosa, D. (2012). Leveraging editor collaboration patterns in Wikipedia. In Proceedings of the 23rd ACM conference on Hypertext and social media (pp. 13–22). New York, NY, USA: ACM.

Shneiderman, B. (2000). Designing Trust into Online Experiences. Commun. ACM, 43(12), 57–59.

Stein, K., and Hess, C. (2007). Does it matter who contributes: a study on featured articles in the german Wikipedia. In Proceedings of the eighteenth conference on Hypertext and hypermedia (pp. 171–174). Manchester, UK: ACM.

Stvilia, B., Twidale, M. B., Gasser, L., and Smith, L. C. (2005). Information quality discussions in Wikipedia. Proceedings of the 2005 international conference on knowledge management, 101–113.

Stvilia, B., Twidale, M. B., Smith, L. C., and Gasser, L. (2008). Information quality work organization in Wikipedia. Journal of the American Society for Information Science and Technology, 1001.

Suh, B., Chi, E. H., Kittur, A., and Pendleton, B. A. (2008). Lifting the veil: improving accountability and social transparency in Wikipedia with wikidashboard. In Proceedings of the SIGCHI Conference on Human Factors in Computing Systems (pp. 1037–1040). New York, NY, USA: ACM.

Suzuki, Y., and Yoshikawa, M. (2012). Mutual Evaluation of Editors and Texts for Assessing Quality of Wikipedia Articles.

Waltinger, U., Breuing, A., and Wachsmuth, I. (2011). Interfacing Virtual Agents With Collaborative Knowledge: Open Domain Question Answering Using Wikipedia-based Topic Models. In T. Walsh (Ed.), (pp. 1896–1902). AAAI Press.

West, R., Weber, I., and Castillo, C. (2012). A data-driven sketch of Wikipedia editors. In Proceedings of the 21st international conference companion on World Wide Web (pp. 631–632). Lyon, France: ACM.

Wilkinson, D. M., and Huberman, B. A. (2007). Cooperation and quality in Wikipedia. In Proceedings of the 2007 international symposium on Wikis (pp. 157–164). New York, NY, USA: ACM.

Zeng, H., Alhossaini, M. A., Ding, L., Fikes, R., and McGuinness, D. L. (2006a). Computing trust from revision history. In Proceedings of the 2006 International Conference on Privacy, Security and Trust: Bridge the Gap Between PST Technologies and Business Services (pp. 1–1). Markham, Ontario, Canada: ACM.

Zeng, H., Alhossaini, M. A., Fikes, R., and McGuinness, D. L. (2006b). Mining Revision History to Assess Trustworthiness of Article Fragments. In Collaborative Computing: Networking, Applications and Worksharing, 2006. CollaborateCom 2006. International Conference on (pp. 1 –10).

Zhao, H., Kallander, W., Gbedema, T., Johnson, H., and Wu, S. F. (2011b). Read What You Trust: An Open Wiki Model Enhanced by Social Context. In SocialCom/PASSAT (pp. 370–379). IEEE.

Author Index